Twayne's United States Authors Series

ERICH FROMM
by Don Hausdorff

ia E. Bowman, *Editor*

INDIANA UNIVERSITY

Since the appearance of *Escape from Freedom* in 1941, Erich Fromm has been one of the most provocative, prolific, and influential thinkers in America. In nineteen books and numerous articles, he has ranged over the fields of psychoanalysis, social psychology, ethical philosophy, religion, economics, and political thought, seeking guidelines for a humanistic theory of man. He has been convinced that traditional wisdom still has validity, but that it must be re-interpreted in accordance with social and intellectual change.

Erich Fromm is the first systematic attempt to survey and analyze the full span of Fromm's ideas, from his first article, on the psychoanalytic meaning of Sabbath ritual, in 1927, through his discussions of character change, Socialism and capitalism, the cold war, and love and destructiveness, to his most recent writings on Mexican villagers and American youth of the 1970's. Particular emphasis is placed on the dialectical, paradoxical turn of Fromm's thought, which is seen as the key to any realistic interpretation of his ideas. *Erich Fromm* also examines the sources of Fromm's methods and concepts, and the critical controversies that have swirled around Fromm's iconoclastic theories.

)R

ssociate Professor of
Jew York University,
grees from Columbia
versity of Minnesota.
erican Civilization,
Science, Modern
ourses at a number of
g Michigan State
sity of Delaware, the
York, and National
aipei, China. He has
scholarly magazines
satire, art, and com-
editing *Literature in
Expansion*.

ERICH FROMM

By DON HAUSDORFF

New York University

(TUSAS) 203

Twayne Publishers :: New York

Preface

PSYCHOANALYST, social theorist and critic, ethical philosopher, teacher and best-selling author: Erich Fromm has been all of these during a long and productive career. As much as any person in our time, he has sought to confront our moral and intellectual dilemmas and to comprehend a humanity that seems resolutely determined to destroy itself. Fromm's work always has been marked by a refusal to yield to the fashionable angst of the twentieth century and by a style that is accessible to educated laymen as well as to scholars. While some critics have deplored both his "optimism" and his popular touch, Fromm is, as Gerald Sykes remarks in *The Hidden Remnant*, one of those people "who actually help make democracy work."

Fromm's ambitious goal, as he told this writer in correspondence, has been to erect "a theory of the various human passions as resulting from the conditions of the existence of man." In pursuit of such a far-reaching theory, he has boldly crossed the boundary lines of familiar fields of knowledge. He has explored the common ground between traditional wisdom and modern experience, between Oriental and Occidental belief systems, between faith and conventional rationalism, between "humanistic" and "scientific" frames of reference. Inevitably, he has drawn anguished cries from some scholars as well as praise from others. Indeed, reading his argumentative critics provides in itself a useful (if sometimes bewildering) introduction to the intellectual ferment of our age.

Now in his seventies, still extremely active, Fromm continues to elude precise classification. When I asked him for a self-definition, he called himself "an atheistic mystic, a Socialist who is in opposition to most Socialist and Communist parties, a psychoanalyst who is a very unorthodox Freudian." In short, no labels quite apply. Like the Spinoza and the Marx he admires, he is an independent and often paradoxical thinker, who strives to be faithful to what he believes are the most humane values of the humane tradition.

Fromm's interests extend into so many fields that most writers who have discussed his work have limited their assessments to one or another specialized aspect: to his Freudian revisionism, for example, or to his philosophy of politics. These restricted approaches are understandable and often useful. But they do considerable injustice to the dialectical, synthesizing turns of Fromm's thought. Recognizing the hazards of an over-all view, I nevertheless have tried in this book to give proper balance to the full range of Fromm's ideas and methods. I am not a specialist in any of the fields under discussion; rather, my own education and experience have ranged widely through the social sciences and humanities. My approach has been one of critical sympathy and intellectual curiosity, and I trust that it has enabled me to obtain the perspective that Fromm's work demands.

The difficulties of organizing such a diversified body of material are obvious. Within the confines of each individual book or article, Fromm's great strength has been his skill in reconciling apparently antithetical approaches to the study of man. But, from work to work, Fromm shifts his focus, sometimes concentrating his energies in one direction, sometimes in another. Some books partially overlap, and some particular discussions have been repeated, with minor or major modifications, several different times. It seems safe to say that Fromm, who shares Emerson's humanistic affirmation as well as his distrust of mechanized man, shares also his organic perspective—and he carries it over into the formulation and presentation of his ideas.

In order to offer a coherent view of Fromm's development as a thinker, while at the same time indicating the range and interrelationships of his ideas, I have tried to effect a compromise between chronological and thematic treatments. Thus, after a short introductory chapter that suggests some of the principal influences on Fromm's attitudes, each chapter is built around a related cluster of ideas that received their greatest emphasis in a given span of time. Within the limited compass of this book, I make no pretense of examining systematically or in depth the ideas of such major and prolific writers as Freud or Marx. But wherever possible I have attempted to supply a sense of background, and of important critical controversies, relevant to the many themes that Fromm has discussed.

DON HAUSDORFF

New York University

Contents

Chronology

1900   Erich Fromm born in Frankfurt, Germany.
1918-   Student, universities of Heidelberg and Munich. Ph.D., Heidel-
1924   berg.
1926   Married Frieda Reichmann. Subsequently divorced.
1929-   Student, Psychoanalytic Institute of Berlin; Lecturer, Psycho-
1932   analytic Institute of Frankfurt and Institute for Social Re-
        search, University of Frankfurt.
1931   *The Development of the Dogma of Christ.*
1932-   With International Institute of Social Research, Geneva.
1933
1934   Emigrated to the United States; became American citizen.
1934-   With International Institute of Social Research, New York
1938   City.
1940-   Guest Lecturer, Columbia University.
1941
1941   *Escape from Freedom.*
1941-   Lecturer, American Institute of Psychoanalysis.
1942
1941-   Faculty, Bennington College.
1950
1943   Married Henny Gurland (died 1952).
1947   *Man for Himself.*
1949   Terry Lecturer, Yale University.
1950   *Psychoanalysis and Religion.*
1951   *The Forgotten Language: An Introduction to the Under-
        standing of Dreams, Fairy Tales, and Myths.* Fellow, Faculty,
        William Alanson White Institute of Psychiatry. Professor of
        Psychoanalysis, National Autonomous University of Mexico;
        Director, Mexican Institute of Psychoanalysis.
1953   Married Annis Freeman.
1955   *The Sane Society.*
1956   *The Art of Loving.*
1957-   Professor, Michigan State University.
1961
1959   *Sigmund Freud's Mission.*
1960   Editor (with D. T. Suzuki and R. De Martino), *Zen Bud-
        dhism and Psychoanalysis.*
1961   *May Man Prevail?*

1962 Professor, New York University. *Marx's Concept of Man.*
Beyond the Chains of Illusion: My Encounter with Marx and
Freud.
1964 *The Heart of Man: Its Genius for Good and Evil.*
1965 Editor, *Socialist Humanism.*
1966 *You Shall Be as Gods: A Radical Interpretation of the Old*
Testament and its Traditions.
1968 *The Revolution of Hope: Toward a Humanized Technology.*
Editor (with Ramon Xirau), *The Nature of Man.*
1970 *Social Character in a Mexican Village* (with Michael Maccoby).
The Crisis of Psychoanalysis.

ERICH FROMM

ERICH FROMM

CHAPTER 1

The Sources of Revision and Synthesis

I *Youth*

TO BEGIN with a truism that some formalistic critics still seem loath to accept, every writer is the product of a particular time and place. The most useful introduction to the ideas of Erich Fromm is some sense of the kind of home in which he grew up and of the intellectual climate that strongly shaped his professional outlook. Frankfurt-on-Main, where Fromm was born on March 23, 1900, was a Prussian city of venerable traditions, whose origins lay back in the first century after Christ. Militant Protestantism, which was preached there as early as 1522, fused comfortably with strong commercial impulses, for reasons that Max Weber, Fromm himself, and others have tried to explain. By the end of the nineteenth century, Frankfurt was one of the leading business and industrial centers of Europe.

Fromm's own family had deep religious roots, but these were Jewish rather than Protestant. His father Naphtali was the son of a rabbi and the grandson of two rabbis. His mother Rosa's family apparently was descended from Russian emigrés who had been converted to Judaism in Finland. One of her uncles, Ludwig Krause, was a Talmudic scholar of considerable reputation.[1] The Fromm household was, therefore, an Orthodox one; and the boy Erich was a close student of the Old Testament. He recalls how, as a boy, he was "exhilarated" by the compassion and the redemptive note struck repeatedly in the stories of Abraham, Adam and Eve, and Jonah, and especially by the prophets Isaiah, Hosea, and Amos: "not so much by their warnings and their announcement of disaster, but by their promise of the 'end of days,' when nations 'shall beat their swords into ploughshares and their spears into pruning hooks: nation shall not lift sword against nation, neither shall they learn war any more.' "[2]

11

Although in later life Fromm abandoned all institutionalized
religion, the ethical substructure and the moral fervor of Old
Testament messianism have remained entrenched in his style
and in his thought. "The first time I heard Fromm," psychoanalyst Rollo May once wrote in *Pastoral Psychology*, "I felt
that here was a man who spoke with the accents of the Hebrew
prophets." In fact, Fromm's evaluation of the impact of Judaism
on Sigmund Freud seems equally applicable to Fromm himself:
"Freud's Jewish background... added to his embrace of the
enlightenment spirit. The Jewish tradition itself was one of
reason and of intellectual discipline, and, besides that, a somewhat despised minority had a strong emotional interest to defeat
the powers of darkness, of irrationality, of superstition, which
blocked the road to its own emancipation and progress."[3]

But the members of Fromm's family were not all seclusive
religious scholars. Jewish families, as well as Protestant ones,
lived in commercial society; it was from a Frankfurt ghetto,
after all, that the Rothschilds arose to found the foremost
banking house in Europe. Naphtali Fromm was an independent
businessman, and Rosa's father was a cigar manufacturer. Apparently, secular and temporal urges did not always mesh equitably
in the family. In Fromm's recollection his household was a tense
one; his father was moody and "over-anxious," and his mother
was "depression-prone."

An only child, Fromm himself was caught up in some of the
same tensions. He feels that he lived in two distinct worlds at
the same time, one which was "pre-modern," Jewish, and traditional, and the other which was the "modern world of industry,
commerce and of finance." Retrospectively, he believes that this
dichotomized existence, almost unbearable in its emotional
polarities, provided the impetus for his own lifelong intellectual
aspirations. As both "stranger" and "participant" in a dynamic,
capitalist society, he felt impelled to create a fresh and viable
synthesis for himself. He could never accept for himself the
role of detached scholar or visionary, of one withdrawn from
the world of practical affairs. But he could also never understand
how a man could consume his energies in making money and
delight in that pecuniary fact.

Fromm has never written very much about the details of his
own life, although ours certainly is an age of candid confession
and some of the most remarkable self-revelations have been

penned by psychoanalysts—following the model of Freud himself. But Fromm, rather than emulating Freud's confessional impulses, seems to have taken seriously Freud's remark that there is "a discretion which one owes to oneself." (In his biography of Freud, Fromm also suggests ironically that Freud himself was not quite so candid as some of his disciples profess to believe.)

In one of his few personal reminiscences in print, Fromm recalls that confusion and dismay at private and public tragedies led him to speculate about fundamental questions. He writes that at the age of twelve he was shocked to learn of the suicide of a beautiful and talented woman, a friend of the family. Such an action, he recalls, seemed both monstrous and incredible.

At thirteen, he commenced a study that he feels provided not only a measure of consolation but also the beginnings of important wisdom. He was introduced to the Talmud by the family scholars. He also studied under the humanistic mystic Rabbi Nehemia Nobel (on whom the writings of Goethe had been a major influence), and under the Hasidic scholar and avowed Socialist Salman Rabinkow. Fromm's Talmudic studies were to continue for fourteen years, until he left organized Judaism. But his interest in religious literature, especially in its ethical and humanistic implications, never ended, and he acknowledges the mystic Meister Eckhart as his favorite author. Moreover, still an atheist after forty years, Fromm at sixty-six devoted an entire book, *You Shall Be As Gods,* to an interpretation of the Old Testament and the Talmudic writings which succeeded it.

Fromm was fourteen when World War I began. Again, he recalls, events almost overwhelmed him. He found himself astonished and "struck with the hysteria of hate" that surged through Germany. Relatives and older friends were killed; his amiable Latin teacher metamorphosed into a fanatic; official propaganda reached frenzied peaks of irrationality and bloodlust. Both sides claimed to be fighting for peace and freedom, and "millions allowed themselves to be slaughtered on both sides for the sake of some territory and the vanity of some leaders."

The end of the war brought comfort to the Frankfurt banking houses; but it also saw the genesis of Nazism, the "curve of horror," as novelist Thomas Pynchon has called it, that began its ascendance under the early Weimar Republic. Fromm, who had pondered the motivations behind suicide and bellicosity, became increasingly interested in political theory and in "the hidden forces which act behind the back of the participants." In 1919 he became a Socialist, although reluctance to engage in practical politics kept him from joining the Socialist party. Instead, he concentrated on formal study at the universities, with special emphasis on sociology and philosophy.

II *The Intellectual Atmosphere*

Perhaps the best way to understand what Fromm studied in those years is to take a brief overview of the intellectual ferment of the early 1920's, especially developments in the social sciences that strongly influenced his thinking. It was a time of extraordinary excitement in the academic community, and Fromm's writings ever since have been studded with references to those ideas and methods. The comprehensive nineteenth-century formulations of Auguste Comte in France, Herbert Spencer in England, and Karl Marx in Germany had achieved international prominence and influence; and they had opened wide the floodgates to the analytical study of human behavior and social institutions. Directly relevant, too, were the biological theories of Charles Darwin, which offered dynamic concepts clustered around the idea of evolution, as well as a demonstration of the persuasive power inherent in the mass accumulation of primary data.

The investigators of industrial, technological society and its roots sought to comprehend it through social, political, and economic "processes"—a term which swept rapidly and pervasively into the scientific vocabulary. In a single chapter of *The Influence of Darwin on Philosophy*, John Dewey used the word "process" no fewer than eight times. And "evolution" itself, supplanting the eighteenth-century concept of "progress," was identified as the methodological key that would unlock the secrets of social processes. No field of study could resist this new concept, from Jakob Burckhardt's scientific history, through the anthropologically oriented "higher criticism" of the Bible that reached its apogee of subtlety in Germany after 1890, to the budding field of psychoanalysis.

One result of the wide diffusion of theories and methods was that, despite the emergence of anthropology, sociology, and psychology as discrete disciplines, there were numerous bridges being built from one field of study to another. The American Lewis Henry Morgan, for example, one of the first modern anthropologists to desert the armchair for "field work," was to have his theories of cultural evolution utilized by Marx and Engels in their studies of the economic organization of the family; later, Freud took cognizance of them in his analysis of primitivism and civilization. Emile Durkheim's concept of "collective representation" (or the "shared idea" of a group of people) was to find its way into German sociology and then into psychoanalytic theory. Marx's impact was enormously wide-ranging and deep. His substitution of material, "objective" situations for Hegel's "idealistic" constructs, his depiction of history in terms of class structure and class struggle, his detailed diagnosis of the capitalistic ethos, and his fusion of voluntaristic and deterministic elements in the social process were to permeate all of the social sciences.

Following the dynamic innovations of Marx, Comte, and Spencer, German sociologists Georg Simmel, Max Weber, and Werner Sombart all sought to relate institutions and concrete facts to value orientations and to the larger social context. They too visualized sociology as a potentially generalizing science of man and, explicitly or implicitly, found a focus in social psychology. The ambitious theoreticians wanted to learn the nature of the *laws* that shaped social institutions and generated human psychologies. Freud, coming from another direction, out of neurology and psychiatry, met the sociologists half-way. All psychology, he once remarked, is social psychology—because all of it is interaction between culture and the individual.

Many theorists still concur with Freud's statement. Hans Gerth and C. Wright Mills have explained the importance of social psychology simply and clearly: "The challenge of social psychology, and its great appeal to modern scholars, is that in a time of intellectual specialization and of social and political disintegration, it promises a view of man as an actor in historical crises, and of man as a whole entity.... The structural and historical features of modern society must be connected with the most intimate features of man's self. That is what social psychology is all about."[4]

III *Psychoanalysis*

Judging from Fromm's subsequent writings, all of these ideas and many of their implications became well known to him during his university studies. The social sciences alone, however, seemed incapable of digging into the roots of individual human behavior. Certainly one of his motives for beginning the study of psychoanalysis, after he received his doctorate from Heidelberg, was that it promised the kinds of answers to human motivations, at deeper levels, that no other field of research offered. Referring back to the suicide episode of his childhood, Fromm has written, "When I became acquainted with Freud's theories, they seemed to be the answer to a puzzling and frightening experience."

Fromm's introduction to psychoanalysis came through didactic analysis in 1925 in Munich, with W. Wittenberg, whose achievements included successful utilization of art as therapy with mute patients. Later Fromm was analyzed by Hanns Sachs (subsequently a biographer of Freud) of the Institute of Berlin. Although Fromm's imagination was aroused because Wittenberg and Sachs, he says, "taught me to turn my attention to the unconscious," he did not feel that either analysis achieved great interpretive success.

Fromm had had no formal medical education when he began his own psychoanalytical training, nor has he had any since. It would be easy to assume that this "gap" in his psychoanalytic education accounted for his later de-emphasis of the physiological roots of personality; some of the critics who have objected to his "de-biologizing" Freud have made precisely this charge. But the matter is complicated. Medical credentials have not always gone hand in hand with a somatic approach to psychoanalytic theory and therapy. Freud's own concepts of the id, ego, and superego bear only the dimmest of resemblances to conventional biology.

Two of the most famous early psychoanalytic schismatics, Alfred Adler and Carl Jung, both disagreed sharply with Freud's sexual, physiological emphasis; so, too, did the "cultural revisionists," Karen Horney and Harry Stack Sullivan, both of whom became associated with Fromm in the 1930's; but all these psychoanalysts had medical degrees. Furthermore, some of Freud's staunchest disciples, none of whom deviated significantly from Freud's instinctual theories, were *not* medically trained. This group included his daughter Anna, and such valued associates as Hanns Sachs, Theodor Reik, and Ernst Kris. Nor, to compound the difficulties of simple cause-and-effect explanation, did Otto Rank have a medical education. Rank's apostasy from Freud was largely attributable to a shift in the *nature* of his biological emphasis. Fromm was setting no precedent, therefore, when he entered psychoanalysis without prior medical education; and he began practicing therapy in Germany as early as 1927.

The United States was to prove, however, a more intractable locale. There, physicians, along with members of other professions, had had a lengthy, arduous struggle to establish standards and licensing procedures as protection against cultists and quacks who for generations had flocked to practice pseudoscientific panaceas. Largely inspired by convictions about professional responsibility, therefore, the American psychoanalysts formed an almost solid wall of resistance against the admission of lay analysts to practice. When Fromm, Theodor Reik, and other experienced analysts emigrated to America in the 1930's, they found that clinical practice was denied to them. "The problem of the lay analyst exiled from Europe," Topeka psychoanalyst Karl Menninger wrote in 1942, "has been an especially painful one." Both Menninger and his brother Roy, highly influential in psychoanalytical groups, made it unmistakably clear on a number of occasions that Fromm's lay status left his qualifications as a psychoanalyst dubious.

Freud's position on this question, outlined in *The Question of Lay Analysis*, needs some clarification because it bears directly on Fromm's own career. Although Freud's researches into psychoanalysis were an outgrowth of his experiences in neurology and psychiatry, he encouraged the training and participation of "lay" analysts. He probably had no choice: rebuffed by the bulk of the medical profession in his efforts to proselytize, he turned elsewhere for converts. His one reservation was that lay analysts should have patients referred to them by medical doctors.

As Freud visualized its future, psychoanalysis was to be more than a "mere handmaid of psychiatry." He believed it could lend insight into art and literature, sociology, philosophy, and many other fields. Apparently, his hope was that specialists from other disciplines would study psychoanalysis and then be in a position to enrich their own fields. Political scientist

Harold Lasswell, for example, studied psychoanalysis and then wrote and lectured widely on the psychopathology of political institutions and politicians themselves. Similarly, Fromm trained in social science and then applied psychoanalytic theory to social institutions and philosophical concepts.

How much medical expertise is necessary for the practicing analyst, other than on questions of referral, remains a moot question. Certainly, the burgeoning of "humanistic" therapies in the 1960's and 1970's raises again a host of medical as well as ethical problems. But one writer, Edgar Friedenberg, has suggested that Fromm's lack of medical training may be an important reason why Fromm's approach to personality problems (unlike that of so many medically trained psychoanalysts) has been "moral and committed, rather than detached and empirical."

Fromm's moral commitment, as indicated earlier, had other sources. Throughout the early 1920's he was still an Orthodox Jew. At twenty, he became a co-founder of the Jüdische Volkschule in Frankfurt—a school which at one time included Martin Buber on its staff. In 1923, still in Frankfurt, Fromm edited a small Jewish newspaper. In 1926, he married Frieda Reichmann, a physician and psychoanalyst who was to obtain a great reputation in her own right, especially for her clinical research with schizophrenic patients; and for some years the Fromms worked collaboratively in a private hospital in Heidelberg. They were divorced later, but he has always acknowledged learning a great deal from her.

In 1927, Fromm, now a practicing analyst and strict Freudian, broke formally with Judaism. With his multiple credentials in social science and psychoanalysis, his background of biblical and Talmudic studies, his early acquaintance with Zen Buddhism, and his strong scholarly ambitions, he began his publishing career. His first article, "Der Sabbath," published in 1927, sought to bring together theories drawn from his highly diversified education. As a complex synthesis focused on an unusual historical-ethical problem, this work presaged in miniature the thrust of all his later work.

CHAPTER 2

The Dialectics of Society and Man

I *The Evolution of Ideology*

FROMM'S article "Der Sabbath" appeared in *Imago,* one of several magazines founded by Freud. In the same year, 1927, Freud published his most systematic exposition—and attempted demolition—of religion, *The Future of an Illusion.* Of Fromm's reverence for the older man's towering reputation there could be no doubt: he cited Freud frequently and uncritically, and he constantly reminded the reader that "Freud has shown us" this or that. Despite such obeisance, Fromm's first article also demonstrated the forthrightness and bold synthesis of methods that would stamp all his future work.

The subject of his article is a historical paradox, the apparently contradictory ordinances that the Bible prescribes for Sabbath observance. "If the Sabbath," Fromm asks, "should be a day of rest and recuperation for man, and if the prohibition of work should function as a good deed and not as a denial, how can we explain some of the prohibitions for this day, which obviously lead to an opposite tendency?"[1] For example, a prohibition like the one against leaving the house seems to be a "burden" rather than a "convenience," and scriptural punishments for Sabbath violations sometimes seem excessively severe. For Fromm, the explanation offered in Exodus, that man should rest because God rested after six days of labor, is anthropomorphic to the point of "blasphemy."

Fromm's own explanation mixes anthropology, philosophy, and psychoanalytic theory. The biblical conception of work, he states flatly, expresses a fundamental relationship between man and nature. The relationship might be literal—economic— or it might be symbolic. In the second instance, Freud's Oedipal construct is seen as helpful: when man, the farmer, "coerces"

19

nature, he is committing a symbolic act of incest against Mother Earth. Elsewhere in the Old Testament, but always in veiled form, such episodes as the father-son conflict in the Garden of Eden suggest that "incestuously determined patricide" was the original crime of mankind. The Bible, says Fromm, suppressed ideas that had been transparently clear in older Babylonian myths.

As opposed to such "sacrificial" prohibitions attached to Sabbath observance, there are also "life-affirming" injunctions. Beginning with Isaiah, the Bible admonishes believers to eat and dress well, to "approach the Sabbath joyfully." To resolve the sacrifice-and-joy contradiction, Fromm employs dialectics. On the one hand, work is connected with punishment through the concept of Original Sin, when man was expelled from the pleasures of Eden ("the womb"). On the other hand, the work-prohibition implies the restoration, at least temporarily, of the "paradise-like, hence workfree-state" for man, *the reconstruction of the harmony of the womb's environment.*

Fromm's reasoning seems both forced and inadequately substantiated, for his metaphors are more grandiose than persuasive. And his language, as he was to confess in later years, is rather clumsily academic. Despite Fromm's reliance on the theories embodied in Freud's *Inhibition, Symptom and Anxiety,* it appears clear that the speculations of Otto Rank and Karl Marx (whom Fromm does not cite) figure strongly in Fromm's interpretation. Rank, in *The Trauma of Birth,* had argued that pre-Oedipal tensions in the newborn baby were crucial. Freud's early reaction to this theory was uncertainty; later, he condemned it. But Fromm's reference to natural states of harmony and disharmony indicates that he was impressed; in later writings, he would modify and expand this conception. As for Marx, his presence, too, can be felt. There is, to be sure, a strong dialectical turn in Freud's thought; but Marx more than Freud seems to have been the likely inspiration for what Fromm calls his own "dynamic explanation for the inner relationship between opposite elements." And Marx more than Freud surely lies behind Fromm's comment about the economic significance of Sabbath prohibition (productivity of labor had to have reached the stage where man could afford the luxury of a work-free day).

In 1929, Fromm moved to Berlin to study at the Psychoanalytic Institute, from which he graduated in 1932. His teachers there included some eminent Freudian scholars: Theodor Reik, Karl Abraham, Sandor Rado, and Franz Alexander. (Freud himself Fromm never met, then or in later years.) Simultaneously, Fromm lectured at several institutes in Frankfurt and continued to write. In his next two important publications, he refined and extended his examination of ideological meanings. He introduced a powerful Marxian weapon of analysis: the dynamics of social class, set inside the conditions of historical change. And, building on the insights of Emile Durkheim, Freud, and others, Fromm began to create his own theory of character formation. As one more mark of his growing independence, he now took direct issue with two of his former teachers, Franz Alexander and Theodor Reik.

In another article that appeared in *Imago*, "The Psychology of the Criminal and of Punishing Society," Fromm concludes that there are fundamentally two kinds of crimes: those that are primarily economic, or "rational-egoistic," in motivation, and others that might be termed "irrational-sexual." These two types are seen as extremes at the ends of a behavioral continuum; most crimes are somewhere in between, the result of a mixture of "libidinal with egoistic strivings." The puzzle, says Fromm, is why most people who are economically underprivileged, and thus unable to gratify perfectly normal wants, do *not* commit crimes.

His answer is a statement of social psychology—society implants certain ideals, enabling most people to prefer poverty to dishonesty. In psychoanalytical terms, some people *do* become criminals because their "superego formation is not all or only imperfectly successful." For the precise mechanisms of unconscious motivation, he refers the reader to *The Criminal, the Judge and the Public*, written in 1928 by psychoanalyst Franz Alexander (later one of the pioneers of psychosomatic medicine) and the criminal lawyer Hugo Staub. Alexander and Staub had diagnosed the etiology of crime through a shrewd Freudian variation on the "social contract" of John Locke and Thomas Jefferson. People, according to this theory, seek to establish equilibrium between the demands of the id and the pressures of the superego; and they make a concession to the social order. Albeit reluctantly, they renounce instinctual needs, hoping for compensatory gratification from society. But they retain the "right of revolution" (as in the Declaration of Independence);

and, when gratification (justice) is not forthcoming, they consider the contract broken. Instinctive drives then operate without restraint.

Alexander and Staub had postulated two kinds of criminals, the "neurotics," whose etiology is primarily psychological, and the "normal" ones, whose etiology is mostly social. Here, Fromm disagrees. "Any unconscious impulse can be extensively rationalized," he insists. "Only the study of the unconscious of the criminal personality can explain." His argument specifically conjoins Marx with Freud: "Sublimation often fails not because of the lack of individual psychic ability, but rather because of the economic circumstances. The proletariat's hostile impulses can leave them 'narcissistically undernourished.'" Thus the question of accountability becomes moot, since both social and psychological pressures are operative and, in fact, fuse.

To Fromm, the archaic penal code persists because the ruling class uses it to bring the masses "in a situation of spiritual ties and dependence on the ruling class, or its representatives, so that they obey and subordinate themselves without the use of force." The values of the ruling class are thus internalized by those who are ruled. One suspects that Franz Kafka would have approved of Fromm's concluding metaphor: "The penal code . . . is the paddle on the wall which shows even the good child that the father is a father and the child a child."

Fromm said recently that in the early 1930's he was still orthodox in his therapeutic practice, still trying to force facts into preestablished theory. His article on crime clearly shows these signs of strain, for Fromm is struggling to incorporate Freud's id-ego-superego psychic topology into his own increasingly radical formulations. Freud regarded psychoanalysis as the potential center of a unified behavioral science, but Fromm now was pointing outward, toward the crucial role of social phenomena in the formation of human personality. Even while he admitted that the ruling class clings tenaciously to its "purposes and prerogatives," he found signs of hope in the evolutionary and increasingly humane tendencies of criminal justice.

But in 1931 he was still asserting his psychoanalytic orthodoxy. In *The Development of the Dogma of Christ,* published that year, he adheres scrupulously to Freud's dictum about the illusions of religion: it is infantile psychic gratification, he says, transferred to collective fantasy. As he now challenged some of

Theodor Reik's ideas, he assured readers that this "opposition certainly does not depend upon any difference in the psychoanalytic presuppositions as such."

Reik had concluded in 1927, in "Dogma and Compulsion," that religion and individual compulsion-neurosis patterns bear startling resemblances. According to Fromm, Reik's "error" was that he tried "to understand people on the basis of a study of dogma," whereas it is necessary "to understand dogma on the basis of a study of people." With a nod to sociologist Georg Simmel, who had rejected the notion of any summary "group" psychology, Fromm maintains that "the social-psychological investigation can study only the character matrix common to all members of the group, and does not take into account the total character structure of a particular individual."[2] Herein lies the kernel of Fromm's "social character" theory, later systematized in *Escape from Freedom* and exemplified experimentally in *Social Character in a Mexican Village*.

To study real people necessitates, for Fromm, appraisal of social and economic facts, rather than a reasoned argument by analogy. His approach in *The Dogma of Christ* is to outline three principal stages of the dogma, from primitive Christianity to the Nicene Council of A.D. 325; to set each stage of belief in historical perspective with a discussion of political and economic conditions (with careful class differentiation); and then to translate each dogmatic concept into psychoanalytic terms. From what conditions did particular dogma originate, and what were the nature and purpose of each "psychic gratification" for believers? In later years, David Riesman cited *The Dogma of Christ* as a clear paradigm of the way Fromm diverged from the classical Freudians on the subject of social issues.[3]

The major points of Fromm's analysis may be summarized briefly. (1) In the Augustan era, the exploited proletarian Jews sought to collaborate with the middle class in a revolt against Rome. When the middle class compromised and revolutionary aims collapsed, the lower-class radicals turned to fantasy for gratification. They gravitated toward a gospel of future judgment which was a compound of internal brotherhood and hatred for the oppressive authorities.

For the suffering masses, the "adoptionist" theory, in which Jesus became the Messiah by a distinct act of God's will, afforded a means of identification: Christ was elevated to God, and "in their unconscious, this crucified god was themselves." In this way, an outlet was also provided for expressing hostility against the father-figure. Finally, the death on the cross expiated the guilt that was inculcated by the death-wish against the father.

(2) By the end of the second century, the Roman Empire had become a "feudal" class-state, with citizenship generally available, and an emperor cult serving to unify the far-flung population. The Roman goal was reconciliation of Christians with the state, and the ruling class itself joined the faith. Christianity lost its revolutionary character, as well as the ethical core that had been expressed through a brotherhood of the oppressed. The ruling class formulated a new dogma of Jesus: man had not become God; rather, God had become man. Jesus now symbolized man's "tender, passive tie to the father." Man should love and submit. Aggressive impulses that once had been directed against authorities now were turned back on the people themselves. Self-annihilation of the Son became the center of Christian dogma.

(3) In the definitive dogma of the Catholic Church, all anti-authoritarian and adoptionist constructions dropped away. The last competitive theory, Arianism, held that God is One, and that the Son was of a different essence. But at Nicaea, Athanasius argued triumphantly that the Son and God shared the essence and whole nature. Unification was completed.

The dogma's tortuous progression through redefinition and crystallization, says Fromm, was the product of men, needs, and changing times. Its convolutions can only be understood dialectically, through an examination of solid facts and unconscious motives. Ten years later, in *Escape from Freedom*, Fromm extended his historical analysis into the Reformation and to modern times—but with some significant changes in his approach to human needs and realities. Twenty years after that, when *The Dogma of Christ* itself was translated and reprinted, Fromm pointed out that he was no longer quite an orthodox Freudian or quite so staunchly an environmentalist. By 1961, even his definition of "ideology" had changed.[4]

But for several more years, after *The Dogma of Christ*, until about 1937, Fromm remained in the fold of faithful Freudians— or at least he so pictured himself. Articles he wrote during these years actually suggested that he was deviating in more and more ways from Freud and that his own theories were beginning to take coherent shape. Freud, by stressing the universality and primacy of the Oedipal sexual triangle, and by insisting that any advanced civilization acted repressively on libidinal drives, had evolved a theory of culture that was almost monolithic. His thinking, as Philip Rieff has suggested in *Freud: The Mind of the Moralist*, really was antihistorical. But Fromm was absorbed with historical change and with the new insights from cultural anthropology; almost everything he wrote in this period intermingled socioeconomic processes with psychodynamics.

Prime examples were "The Theory of Mother Right and its Relevance for Social Psychology" and an essay on Robert Briffault's book *Mothers,* where Fromm began assembling his ideas on the mythological and sociological implications of matriarchal theory. Fromm had touched on this topic when discussing "incest" in his Sabbath article; now he underlined its significance by arguing that "the psychic basis of the Marxist social program was predominantly the matricentric complex." These ideas will be discussed more fully in conjunction with *The Forgotten Language,* which Fromm wrote in 1951, outlining his own post-Freudian version of the meaning of the Oedipus legend and of Sophocles' trilogy.

On several occasions in the 1930's Fromm delivered direct attacks on familiar concepts of, and attitudes about, Freud himself. In "The Social Background of Psychoanalytic Therapy," he said that Freud was not, widespread belief to the contrary, liberal toward sex; Freud's philosophy actually was "puritanical." This theme he would later develop in *Sigmund Freud's Mission* (1959). In "The Method and Function of an Analytical Social Psychology," Fromm argued that socioeconomic changes not only could act as potent determinants of individual behavior—they might modify the instinctual structure itself. Freud, he says, rejected the idea of a "social instinct," while Marx "did not go into any detail about the quality of various drives and needs." But he was certain that Marxism and psychoanalysis were not irreconcilable, and that critics like Bertrand Russell, who argued that the Freudian "drive for love" and the Marxian "drive for money" represented an unbridgeable polarity misinterpreted the thrust and depth of both thinkers.

Because "instinctual structure" continued to occupy a prominent place in Fromm's formulations, his positions during these years won favor with some writers who felt that Freud was fundamentally on the right track. A striking example was Herbert Marcuse, himself a highly independent theorist who also sought to bridge Freud and Marx. Assessing Fromm's articles of the 1930's, Marcuse praised his "valuable service" in bringing to light the "latent" sociological critique in Freud. Fromm, he said, had vividly demonstrated the link between socioeconomic and instinctual structures; this demonstration was valuable because "sharpening of the psychoanalytical concepts means sharpening their critical function, their opposition to the prevailing form of society."[5] Marcuse's estimate of Fromm was to turn increasingly negative as Fromm gradually became identified with two sharp revisionists of Freudian theory, Karen Horney and Harry Stack Sullivan. By the late 1930's, Fromm no longer considered himself a strict Freudian in theory or therapy.

II "Neo-Freudianism"

Asked in 1966 about his connection with "Neo-Freudianism," Fromm replied, "I've never actually been happy about that label." Aside from personal reasons (Fromm always has preferred to think of himself as a completely independent thinker, rather than as a member of any "school"), Fromm is correct in believing that the term is imprecise. But ever since he settled in the United States in the 1930's and began his association with two other psychoanalysts, fellow German emigré Karen Horney and American Harry Stack Sullivan, the label "Neo-Freudian" has been applied to all three; and it has stuck.

They worked together and they obviously learned a great deal from one another. They concurred in disputing the efficacy of Freud's "dispassionate" mode of administering psychoanalytic therapy. While they agreed with Freud about the importance of childhood experience and trauma, they stressed more than he did the importance of problems derived from adult experience. Above all, they shared a belief that Freud overestimated the role of "instincts" in personality formation; and, in fact, they rejected the Freudian concept of human instinct altogether. All three placed greater emphasis on the critical role played by social and cultural factors, on what Sullivan called "interpersonal relations."

Despite these similarities, "Neo-Freudianism" was a vague and somewhat misleading term. In the first place, it blurred important distinctions in temperament and method, distinctions which became more apparent in later years. In the case of some other psychoanalysts who have been called "Neo-Freudians," Abram Kardiner and Franz Alexander for example, fundamental differences have been even more profound. Besides, the path of psychoanalytic theory has been so convoluted that influences have gone in many directions: there are consequential ways in which Fromm has more in common with Carl Jung or Wilhelm Reich, for instance, than with Horney or Sullivan. And finally, the word itself, "Neo-Freudian," seems to connote more a revival of Freud's ideas than an attempt to make major changes in Freudian theory. It would fit more appropriately the celebrants of Freudian orthodoxy in the 1950's and 1960's. But, to repeat, the term has stuck. Fromm himself has used it unapologetically in an article on the history of psychoanalysis, and a recent, sophisticated, and generally sympathetic account of Fromm, Horney, Sullivan, Kardiner, and Alexander (and Harold Lasswell), places the term squarely in the title.[6] Therefore, it is worthwhile to examine briefly what is meant by the "social" revision of Freud and to glance at the general formulations of Horney and Sullivan.

Freud himself instituted the study of the relationship between the individual and society as early as 1913 in *Totem and Taboo,* and he made other contributions in such later works as *Group Psychology and the Analysis of the Ego* and *Civilization and Its Discontents.* The "ego," which Freud defined as that aspect of the self which tests reality, became the center of an almost special field of study inside psychoanalysis, as developed by such faithful Freudians as Heinz Hartmann, Anna Freud, and Ernst Kris. "Ego-psychology" was one cornerstone in the socializing of psychoanalysis, although Fromm recently (in "The Crisis of Psychoanalysis") charged that Hartmann and his colleagues have distorted some of Freud's most significant, and radical, concepts.

Freud, however, always insisted on the primacy of instinctual drives even though his later work emphasized "life" and "death" drives at the expense of the id-ego-superego group of concepts. The Freudian "id" (based on Georg Groddeck's *Es,* or "It"), was a "seething cauldron" of undifferentiated desires. The id demanded gratification at all costs, while society demanded subordination of individualistic to group needs; and the result was an inevitable, and interminable, tug of war. Without civili-

zation, man was a savage beast; but the price of civilization—
any civilization—was neurosis, anxiety, depression. Erotic drives
and conflicts were basic in this scheme, although sex was hardly,
despite the assertions of many popularizers and critics, the sum
total of Freudian theory.

Some of Freud's early followers, absorbing ideas either from
the rapidly developing social sciences or from their own clinical
observations, or both, disagreed about fundamental points.
Alfred Adler in particular (for motives which apparently included his own personal sense of inferiority and his strong
political convictions) abandoned the instinctual-sexual core of
personality theory. Adler substituted as guiding human motives
the quest for, and frustration of, power. He was not especially
sophisticated in sociology, but his "style of life" concept, his
awareness of the significance of social status and the need for
"recognition by others" were important bridges toward a new,
dynamic psychology. "We cannot comprehend the psychic activities," Adler said, "without at the same time understanding...
social relationships." Adlerians still argue heatedly, and with
justification, that his ideas were influential on writers like Horney
and Fromm.[7]

Another important early progenitor of interpersonal theory
was Wilhelm Reich. His *Character Analysis* (1933) was the
first really systematic study of "character traits" as the product
of interaction between the individual and society. "Every social
order," wrote Reich, "creates those character forms which it
needs for its preservation. . . . it is a matter of a deep-reaching
process in each new generation, of the formation of a psychic
structure which corresponds to the existing social order, in all
strata of the population."

Now Fromm moved to America in 1934 when the Institute
for Social Research, for which he had been working in Geneva,
transferred its headquarters to New York City. Since Fromm,
Horney, and Sullivan soon began working together, their efforts
have sometimes been called the "Americanization" of psychoanalysis. But some of the purely German roots have already
been described, and the Fromm-Horney-Sullivan triumvirate
was two-thirds German to begin with: the theories of Fromm
and Horney had acquired important "social" dimensions before
either emigrated to the United States. No question, however,
but that these theories did find fertile soil here, in the form of

American social and economic conditions, and in the pre-existence of a substantial body of knowledge in the social sciences. As one writer has phrased it, these factors "gave the revisionists the impulse, the possibility, and the model for their subsequent development."[8]

Karen Horney had taught for many years at the Psychoanalytic Institute in Berlin, as had Wilhelm Reich. As early as 1924, she was bluntly criticizing Freud's blatantly masculine biases; and she shortly became the most original contributor to a sophisticated psychoanalytic theory about women as women (not, as Freud seemed to believe, as men without penises). Quite likely, she was an important influence behind Fromm's rejection of Freud's "anti-feminism," although not necessarily the *major* influence. At any rate, it is interesting that in the 1960's Fromm declared that Freud's greatest single error was his psychoanalytic theory about women.[9]

In disputing Freud on this point, Horney stressed the role of environmental conditioning in shaping women's "feminine" approach to life. She found persuasive documentation in the findings of the new cultural anthropology. Edward Sapir urged in 1930 a fusion of insights among the various social sciences, and the succeeding decade witnessed an outpouring of cross-cultural studies from Margaret Mead, Ralph Linton, Ruth Benedict, Clyde Kluckhohn, and others. All these writers (sometimes themselves called "Neo-Freudian Anthropologists") offered evidence about the wide range of effects that different cultures could have on individual psyches.

The implications went beyond "female" psychology: the very concept of "normality" was called into question. And, if "normality" was a relative conception, by what standards could anyone identify "neurosis"? When Horney turned to examining "actual life conditions," she abandoned one cardinal Freudian tenet after another. She jettisoned Freud's "biologism," including libido theory—the notion of a fixed quantity of available "energy" that might be directed inward or outward. She challenged his dualistic tendencies, his mechanistic approach to human relationships, and his sternly amoral attitude toward patients.

In *The Neurotic Personality of Our Time* (1937), Horney diagnosed Western capitalism, especially in its virulent American form, as a breeding ground for neurotic competitiveness ("neurotic" because it generated excessive rigidity and also thwarted people's abilities to reach their "potential"). Children everywhere, she said, were born with a love-and-fear ambivalence; and the way the balance swung depended mostly upon cultural attitudes as transmitted through the family. Life was largely a series of conflicting tendencies to move towards, against, or away from people. Conflicts of this kind bred "anxiety," and the need to fend off anxiety feelings led to the formation of "escape mechanisms."

But given ample love, she argued, the worst of this struggle might be ameliorated. Despite the primacy of childhood experience, situational factors kept changing; her therapy became increasingly oriented toward dealing with the patient's perception of the world in the here and now—too much so, ultimately, for Sullivan and his followers. Aside from Horney's optimism (which was never as ingenuous as her detractors made out) and her apparent emphasis on examining "consciousness" rather than probing "unconsciousness," she raised other problems for more traditional colleagues and critics.

In confronting an old psychotherapeutic problem, the lengthy time spent in analysis, she sought ways to shorten the duration of treatment, and even made a serious attempt to justify "self-analysis." Such an idea was, of course, horrifying to those who believed that the analyst's couch and the laborious pursuit of buried meanings were the very soul of therapy. Horney was accused of oversimplifying complexities, of offering "lending-library psychoanalysis," and of making "social adjustment" a fashionable and accessible accessory for the troubled middle class.

How many of Horney's ideas run parallel to Fromm's should become obvious in later chapters of this book. Points of divergence he himself has identified on several occasions. He found her "social" theory too general and inadequately grounded in clear conceptions of social class or of historical change. He thought she accepted "cultural relativism" too uncritically, and that she never explained where she believed an individual's "potential" came from. She herself, after moving disputatiously from institute to institute and finally founding her own, died in 1952.

As for Harry Stack Sullivan, nobody ever accused him of oversimplification. Even his ardent admirers admit that he was one of the worst writers in the history of psychoanalytic thought. The language problem with Sullivan was not the mystical and pseudomystical diffuseness that chokes much of the writing of Carl Jung and Otto Rank; his difficulty was an overspecialized, super-technical preciseness. Unlike Horney (and, to a large extent, Fromm), Sullivan always addressed himself to his peers, assuming their intimate familiarity with the terminology of social psychology and of physiology. His books and papers, so the Sullivan cliché goes, breathe "the odor of the clinic."

Such a style of low-level concreteness is as unfortunate for most readers as are the high-level abstractions of many philosophers and literary critics. But it is understandable since, as with Frieda Fromm-Reichmann, Sullivan's theoretical schemes were rooted directly in clinical experience; and they are always related closely to that hermetic world. A student of William Alanson White and Adolf Meyer in America, Sullivan's first success came with "reaching" schizophrenic patients. (Freud had discounted the possibility of fruitful therapy with them.) From clinical tests and observations, Sullivan built his "interpersonal theory" of psychiatry.

Up to a point, Sullivan's general theory of human experience paralleled Karen Horney's. Experience is perpetual, he said: from birth onward, every individual is establishing contact with, "inter-acting" with, absorbing attitudes from, reacting to, others. But he pursued interaction to its ultimate implications. In an important sense, he concluded, men *are* their experience. As Sullivan conceived it, following on the speculations of American social-psychologist George Herbert Mead, "self" is not really an entity so much as it is a dynamism, originating and functioning "interpersonally."

Sullivan emphasized the "wholeness" of personality; but, like Horney, he never fully systematized its workings. He bifurcated human purposes, for example, into (1) the pursuit of satisfactions (which were directly associated with bodily organization) and (2) the pursuit of security. All these strivings are basically biological; but they are shaped, immediately and continually, by parental judgments, examples, teachings. This cultural conditioning of raw biological material so fuses heredity and environment that the terms really have no separate meanings at all.

His theory then blends social psychology still further with

physiology. As childhood conflicts develop between personal strivings and culturally approved patterns, anxiety develops; and it brings concomitant somatic manifestations. Conversely, purely physiological needs—hunger and stomach contractions, for instance—breed anxieties with psychological components. Hence Sullivan, like such psychosomatic theorists as Franz Alexander, Flanders Dunbar, and Hans Selye, stressed the permanent interaction of psyche and soma: the individual is biosocial and inextricably bound up with culture and its derivatives.

There really was no place in Sullivan's scheme for Freud's instinct and libido theories. Even such key Freudian terms as "preconscious" and "unconscious" processes were transposed by Sullivan into "selective inattention" and "disassociation," conceptions that were, presumably, less metaphysical and more accessible to clinical investigation, diagnosis, and therapy.

Again, some parallels between Sullivan and Fromm become evident later in this book—parallels that Fromm points out over the years. That he never shared Sullivan's predilection for intensive clinical investigation seemed less important to Fromm than their agreement on the significance of "inter-personal" relations and their separate quests for human "wholeness." Fromm held important positions at both Sullivan institutes, the William Alanson White Institute and the Washington School of Psychiatry.

Fromm's major disagreement with Sullivan's ideas came years later, after Sullivan's death (1949) and the posthumous publication of Sullivan's later writings. Both men developed dynamic theories of "self," but Fromm came to believe that the Sullivan version was totally swallowed up in the "socialization" process. Sullivan had become a victim, Fromm felt by 1955, of the very conditions he was trying to describe. For Fromm, a truly "objective" theory required the addition of historical and philosophical perspectives. But these estimates were to come later. In the late 1930's, Fromm was still working out his own theories step by step; and his first two American articles, "The Social Philosophy of 'Will Therapy'" and "Selfishness and Self-Love," both appeared in 1939 in Sullivan's journal, *Psychiatry*.

III   *Social Character*

Fromm's two 1939 articles examined some implications of the psychotherapist's role and the nature and meaning of love relationships. Both, therefore, were concerned with mental health and both took sharp issue with conventional psychoanalytic attitudes. "Will therapy" was the name Otto Rank had given to his own psychoanalytic approach; and Fromm, in "The Social Philosophy of 'Will Therapy,'" scrutinized not only Rank's special premises but also the premises of *any* therapist. No therapist, he argues, can be totally "objective" with a patient. Inevitably, psychoanalysts are subjective about such basic concepts as "health" and "neurosis." Surely, he says, the psychoanalyst's own social philosophy importantly influences his therapeutic method and his conception of what constitutes "cure."

In "Selfishness and Self-Love," Fromm took a fresh look at a problem that had plagued philosophers for centuries: what is the relationship between love for oneself and love for other people? After glancing at what Calvin, Kant, Freud, and others had commented, Fromm concludes that the familiar polarity between "self" and "others" is false. There is such a thing as "narrow self-interest," and it is indeed antithetical to loving anyone else; but it is equally opposed to one's "true" self-interest. For a paradigmic statement of this point, he cites Spinoza: "The more each person is able to seek his profit, that is to say, to preserve his being, the more virtue does he possess." The key lies in the interpretation of the word "profit." Conceived narrowly, as *material* interests, it sets up barriers against personal growth as well as against deep feelings for other people. Fromm's Spinozan outlook strikingly parallels that of Martin Buber, the Jewish theologian and philosopher whom he had admired in his youth;[10] for the psychological base on which Fromm's argument rests is that a person needs the capacity to love before *any* love can take place. To "love oneself" is to affirm humanness, a quality that is the necessary precursor to loving another. The other loved one then can become an "incarnation of essentially human qualities."

The theoretical positions taken in these articles were extremely important for Fromm's later work. Herbert Marcuse has stressed the seminal significance of the point about the analyst's "subjectivity"; in recent years, the unorthodox psychoanalyst Thomas Szasz has pushed the relativistic implications of the idea still farther. Fromm himself has incorporated the passages from "Selfishness and Self-Love" into several subsequent books, and they are intrinsic in his more extended discussions of both "the self" and "love."

In both articles, Fromm blended his theoretical discussion with references to immediate practical applications. He felt that "will therapy," which had gained considerable popularity among certain occupational groups, represented a dangerously authoritarian direction. He felt that misconceptions about "self-love" and "self-interest" had become increasingly pervasive and increasingly destructive. And he issued stern warnings on both counts—as later discussions of these implications indicate.

In other words, even as Fromm was developing the ideas that became integrated into his total theory, he was evidencing deep concern about contemporary events and their ethical consequences. This fusion of purposes had always been present in Fromm's work, but it was becoming more apparent in the late 1930's. For some critics, the fusion has been one of his great strengths; for others, there has been altogether too much strain between his scientific ambitions and his humanitarian presuppositions. Some have insisted, in fact, that Fromm's science has collapsed under the weight of his ethical imperatives. Fromm tends to reject the polarity itself, for he does not see "science" and "ethics" as totally distinct worlds of discourse since the unifying factors are man himself and the totality of his relationship to nature.

Fromm was working to create a systematic "theory" at this time: but, as he wrote in 1941, the press of political events necessitated a revision of his approach and of his time schedule. He was forced to "interrupt" his primarily theoretical efforts because of the immediately threatening phenomenon of totalitarianism. Over the ensuing years, the "theory" did emerge, although in piecemeal form. But in 1941 he gathered some largely completed phases of his theory and used them to examine an urgent topical problem: "freedom." The resulting book, *Escape from Freedom*, is a remarkably ingenious blend of purposes, as well as of techniques. Ironically, the unexpected focus of "freedom" ultimately became the center of his theoretical conceptions anyway. In this sense, since he was building on directly "practical" considerations, Fromm demonstrated clearly just how "organic" a thinker he was.

In *The Dogma of Christ* in 1931, with its intermingled analysis of human needs, systems of belief, and socioeconomic data,

Fromm had already demonstrated his nascent methodology. Formal ideologies, he had argued in that book, really were the social and political equivalents of individual rationalizations; and he had tried to explain, by historical example, the process by which the private had been translated into the public. In a 1932 article, Fromm employed the terminologies of both Freud and Marx to explain the kind of process he was trying to systematize. His objective, he said, was "to understand the instinctual apparatus of a group, its libidinous and largely unconscious behavior, in terms of its socioeconomic structure."[11]

By 1941, with almost a decade of additional work and thought behind him, Fromm was ready to present a more comprehensive explanation of his method. *Escape from Freedom* embodied the method, which he called "social character," inside an analysis of modern institutional and ideological evolution. Its theoretical form was outlined in an appendix to the book. Any given society, Fromm explains, transplants through all of its "educational" mechanisms a cluster of values, beliefs, and modes of operation. Inevitably, most members of a group acquire a large number of traits of a substantially similar nature. These shared aspects of character, which are a selection of social possibilities and which never constitute all of any particular individual's traits, he calls the "social character." He defines it as "the essential nucleus of the character structure of most members of a group which has developed as the result of the basic experiences and mode of life common to that group."[12]

"Essential nucleus," Fromm says; therefore, man is "primarily a social being," one who is "historically conditioned." But he emphasizes that he is not posing a polarity of cultural-versus-biological determinants. He concurs with Harry Stack Sullivan's argument that the question "heredity-or-environment?" is artificial and meaningless; the one functions always and inseparably inside the other. Indeed, Fromm's theory is partially predicated on assumptions that seem to resemble those of Horney and Sullivan. Like Horney, he speaks of "potentials" at birth; like Sullivan, he refers to an original human "dynamism" that undergoes a reciprocal and continuing interrelationship with society. But Horney, Fromm has observed, was vague about "potentials"; and Sullivan, he has remarked in recent years, seems to have postulated a "dynamism" in which the self itself totally dissolves.

Fromm insists that there are human *needs,* which exist apart
from the obviously physiological drives, and are present prior to
any socializing process. He calls them "psychological qualities,"
and he cites the most crucial as "tendencies to grow, develop
and realize potentialities." These needs, he says, are psychologically equivalent to "identical biological tendencies." A tendency
to grow, for example, leads to the "desire for freedom and hatred
against oppression." Thomas Jefferson's maxim about man's "in-
alienable rights," which serves as one of several epigraphs intro-
ducing *Escape from Freedom,* is thus more than political
philosophy for Fromm; it is, he suggests, "founded in inherent
human qualities."

"Human nature" is, of course, an ambiguous and much-abused
term. Although Fromm is well aware how the term has been
invoked to justify any favored political, economic, or social
policies, he nevertheless finds it useful. It becomes a dynamic
concept that internalizes certain elements of social structure,
and also (as Marx insisted) a counter-force lending its own
impetus to social evolution. In "social character" theory, this
human dynamism-in-social-context replaces "mechanistic Freudian biologism," vague metaphysics, and rigid "pseudo-Marxian"
socioeconomic determinism.

Freud was correct, says Fromm, to stress the paramount role
of the family as the "psychological agent of society," but Freud
was wrong when he assumed that instinctive (and primarily
sexual) drives are both the root of cultural phenomena and the
core of permanent hostility to cultural "suppressions." And Max
Weber was also wrong, Fromm says, in postulating an "idealistic"
theory of social effects. Emphasizing the power of ideas on
individuals and societies is well and good, but he feels that
Weber, like Marx, lacks a psychological dynamic. The power
of ideas is effective, Fromm says, only when the ideas "are
answers to specific human needs prominent in a given social
character."

Fromm argues that social character theory makes it possible
to see how the social process actually works. As the individual's
needs and drives merge with a social consensus through the
internalization of group values, he is led "to act according
to what is necessary for him from a practical standpoint and
also to give him satisfaction from activity psychologically."
From the society's perspective, "the social character internalizes

external necessities and thus harnesses human energy for the
task of a given economic and social system." (Passages like these
exemplify what one critic has called Fromm's "dazzling" ability
to "mirror" one set of perspectives inside another. It was the
kind of analysis Fromm was to perform in later books with many
different sets of perspectives.)

A logical inference can be drawn from the social character
theory. If and when a society's needs and purposes mesh perfectly with the psychological-physiological needs "inherent"
in man, a reasonable facsimile of utopia would have arrived.
The tragedy of man's history, Fromm confesses, is that agreement on societal purposes has not been achieved. And he admits
that much remains obscure: "We are not yet able to state clearly
in psychological terms what the exact nature of this human
dynamism is." In *Man for Himself,* six years later, he was to
attempt a more exact formulation. For now, he was certain
only that "relatedness" was the key problem of psychology.
Alfred Adler would have agreed completely.

The psychoanalytic root of the entire process was the Freudian concept of the "superego," the third unit in Freud's tri-
partite scheme of the mind. The id made its unreasonable demands, the ego made contact with the outside world, and the
superego (which was fundamentally the parental distillation
of the world's attitudes) acted as censor and censurer. In the
process of "socializing" Freud during the 1930's and 1940's,
several psychoanalysts had expanded the nature and function
of the superego concept—sometimes, as Fromm did, abandon-
ing the term itself.

Most closely related to Fromm's "social character" adaptation
was the "basic personality" theory of Abram Kardiner, which
he outlined most definitively in *The Individual and His Society*
(1946). Despite some differences in terminology, Kardiner's
theory matches Fromm's in many respects; and Kardiner gives
credit to Fromm for pioneering research in this area. But Kardiner has always hewed a line closer to the original ideas of
Freud, although he became a serious student of the same cultural anthropology that helped influence Horney and Fromm.
The gulf between Kardiner and Fromm has widened perceptibly
over the years as Fromm gradually expanded his interpretation of human "needs" and the "self."

The introduction of fundamental human "needs," inciden-

tally, represented a major change from Fromm's earlier exposition of social and psychological dynamics; for no such idea is
explicit in his work of the early 1930's. The most obvious explanation for the change, and the one offered most often by sympathetic as well as hostile critics, is that Fromm reacted to public
events. Martin Birnbach writes, for example, that Fromm was
even more a cultural relativist in the 1930's than Kardiner. But
cultural relativism seemed morally inadequate in the face of
the newly barbaric cultures of the Axis powers. "This writer
would guess," says Birnbach, "that a comparatively objective
methodology left Fromm no ground on which to base an unfavor-
able judgment of the social character that proved so receptive
to totalitarianism in Nazi Germany."[13]

Birnbach's guess is a sensible one, and it unquestionably contains part of the truth. The advent of Nazism, Fromm has said
many times, greatly affected his thinking on important questions.
But Fromm has mentioned other considerations as well which
relate to his own background and to his clinical experience.
Before examining those factors, which Fromm was to explain a
few years hence, it is worth turning to his analysis of the
advent of totalitarianism—an analysis that culminates in *Escape
from Freedom.*

IV *The Authoritarian Threat*

By Fromm's own reckoning, his interest in political behavior
extends back to World War I, when he felt horrified at the
upsurge of irrational belief and action. By the end of the 1920's,
it was apparent that German unrest was deep and portentous:
the republic was shaky, and swastika armbands were multiply-
ing. Under the general auspices of the International Institute
for Social Research, Fromm, with psychoanalyst Ernest Schachtel and others, initiated a study in 1929 that tried to assess what
was happening. This study, "Character of German Workers and
Employees in 1929/30," had clear political implications. "We
wanted," Fromm recalls, "to ascertain what the chances were
for Hitler's being defeated by the majority of the population."
Presumably, most Germans were inclined more toward democracy than Nazism, but how deeply were these opinions rooted?
Would Germans go so far, for example, as to fight for democratic
beliefs, or would they yield to authoritarianism under pressure
—suggesting that their *deeper* values lay elsewhere?[14]

Open-ended questionnaires were designed to elicit "unintended, unconscious" responses. A sample question was "Which men in history do you admire most?" If a worker answered Alexander, Caesar, or Napoleon, the answer was interpreted as indicating "authoritarian" bias. If he responded Socrates, Pasteur, or Kant, he was classified as "democratic." If Marx or Lenin appeared in the responses, classification depended on the company they kept. After these detailed questionnaires were administered in Frankfurt to about six hundred persons, the investigators concluded that about 10 percent of the workers and employees surveyed had an "authoritarian character structure"; about 15 percent had a "democratic character structure"; the remaining considerable majority lay somewhere in between. The results seemed to indicate that no great sympathy for Nazism would be found among the German working class, but also that the degree of absolute hostility was not very profound.

This investigation was certainly one of the earliest into the psychology of Nazism; among the later researchers were Harold Lasswell, the psychoanalytically trained political scientist, whose examinations of middle-class appeals were first published in 1933, and Siegfried Kracauer, whose imaginative book, *From Caligari to Hitler: A Psychological Study of the German Film,* appeared in 1947. The Frankfurt study was also theoretically important as a pioneering effort toward the concept of the "authoritarian character," one to be more fully developed in *The Authoritarian Personality* by T. W. Adorno and others.

In America in the 1930's, Fromm, like many of his colleagues in psychoanalysis, social psychology, and anthropology, was highly critical of many quasi-democratic institutions. Bureaucracy, regardless of its ideological rationale, was hardly an ideal structure for breeding independent thought and action. Competitive society, as Karen Horney argued in 1937, wreaked havoc on the psyches of winners and losers alike.

In this climate of anxiety, in 1939, with the Nazi explosion into war imminent, Fromm attacked Otto Rank's "will therapy." Rank's premise, said Fromm, was the supremacy of belief: "What I will is true . . . what I want to believe." In the therapeutic situation, the analyst ("the superior man") becomes the voice of reality, an "assistant ego," to direct the submissive patient. Fromm felt that this psychiatric approach had a political counterpart—the authoritarian line that extended from Nietzschean arrogance to Hitler's opportunistic relativism, manipulation of language and ideas for purposes of power, and a conviction that injustice and suffering are inherent in human existence. More disturbing than Rank's theory itself was its growing popularity among various groups, especially social workers. If Fascist philosophy shed its overt political symbols, Fromm speculated, its "quick, easy solutions" offered an irresistible appeal to many troubled people. For social workers struggling with virtually insoluble economic problems, says Fromm, the Rank theory that one can convert illusions into Absolute Truth is a glittering panacea. (In this connection, one might note the spate of sociological analyses during the 1940's and 1950's which argued, on almost identical grounds, that Superman comics and Mickey Spillane novels derived much of their appeal from their advocacy of swift, "no-nonsense" vengeance.)

By 1941, when Fromm published *Escape from Freedom,* the Western European democracies were at war with Germany and Italy. Certainly, Nazism was the most brutal ideology loose in the world. But for years Fromm had been stressing not only the Nazi threat but also the susceptibility to authoritarian ideas of people living under "democratic" capitalism. One of the most noteworthy features of *Escape from Freedom* was that Fromm, militantly anti-Nazi, also confronted directly the problem of why people gravitated toward authoritarianism in *any* modern setting.

The basic questions were about human "freedom": How had the meanings of that ambiguous word shifted as the Western world moved from closed feudal order to the relatively open-class society of mid-twentieth century? How could one account for human tendencies to seek, or retreat from, individual freedom? Among other things, Fromm was attempting in this multi-sided book a psychoanalytic interpretation of history. In this respect, *Escape from Freedom* was in part a sequel to *The Dogma of Christ* and in part a precursor to the analysis of "cold war" ideologies and anxieties that he was to present years later in *May Man Prevail?*[15]

Freud had also subjected history to the psychoanalytic eye. But, Fromm argues, by clinging to the conception of virtually fixed instincts that are either satisfied or frustrated, Freud failed to comprehend the psychic significance of historical change. For Fromm, there are "certain definite changes of man's character

[that] take place from one historical epoch to another": the "spirit" of the Middle Ages, of the Renaissance, and of the stages of capitalism are all quite different. The "spirit" of an age leads Fromm to character structure and to the explication of "social character" as a mechanism for understanding the relation between individual growth and historical evolution. Freedom, he says, can best be understood as a series of biological, social, and historical dialectical processes.

Human individuation, in Fromm's theory, begins with the severing of the umbilical cord. Then other primary ties are cut: from the mother as total provider, from nature, from the clan, the caste, the church. Each new grasp of biological and social autonomy brings a growth in self-strength but simultaneously a new kind of aloneness, and of fear. So liberation and frustration are the joint consequences of each bold step into a brave, but dangerous, new world. As the individual's power of reason and sense of independence grow, so too do the possibilities of insecurity and of what Fromm on an earlier occasion had described as a "feeling of powerlessness." The history of man, too, is seen as a process of evolutionary individuation, following an equally dialectical course. The gradual freedom from restrictive social ties, coupled with the "lack of possibilities for the positive realization of freedom and individuality," have created the dilemma of modern man.

Fromm's historical outline to some degree parallels the pattern of *The Dogma of Christ*, but it is wider in range and includes the new factor of "basic human needs." He begins with the Renaissance and Jakob Burckhardt. With minor reservations, he follows that scholar's interpretation of the distinctions between Medieval and Renaissance "spirit," and of the dynamics involved. Medieval man had limited mobility and choice, but he maintained some "concrete" individualism in that he possessed ways to express himself in his work and in his emotional life. As social stratification eroded, he began to develop greater "self-awareness as an individual."

Incipient capitalism, in its turn, generated class mobility, individual self-reliance, and new roles for capital, the market, and competitive energies. The additional erosion of clear-cut socioeconomic structures, however, meant that greater independence was coupled with new insecurities. With Max Weber, R. H. Tawney, and Werner Sombart now among his chief

sources, Fromm examines the way in which Protestantism prepared man to play a role in the new capitalistic system. The
catalysts of that preparation were the two great Protestant reformers, Martin Luther and John Calvin. Both, says Fromm,
were authoritarian personalities and thoroughly unpleasant
people. Luther has always been a favorite subject for psychoanalytic interpreters: in recent years, Erik Erikson (*Young Man
Luther*) and Norman O. Brown (Chapter XIV, "The Protestant
Era," in *Love Against Death*) have both tried to assess the
"inner meaning" of Protestantism through Luther's personality.
Fromm's Luther preached love for God, but he really appealed
(through the "unconscious") for submission to a higher power.
Simultaneously, Luther urged freedom from unconscionable
church authorities—even while he thundered that man was
essentially powerless. The result, says Fromm, was a psychologically disabling merger of love and surrender.

In an article in 1939, "Selfishness and Self-Love," Fromm
had already accused Calvin of urging an ethic that stressed
humility to the point where it reached unbearable self-contempt.
Now, "social character" theory extends that ethic's implications.
The Calvinist turned of necessity to compulsive activity, and
effort became an aim in itself. This aim, Fromm argues, was
"the most important psychological change which has happened
to man since the end of the Middle Ages. . . . men came to be
driven to work not so much by external pressure but by an
internal compulsion." Here then is Max Weber's Protestant Ethic,
supplied with a psychological base to help explain the formation of a new social character. For external restraint, protestant-
ized man substituted a "slavedriver conscience," reformulated
three hundred-odd years later as the Freudian superego.

Under the capitalistic ethos, says Fromm, man did gain new
economic and political freedoms, steps toward a positive self.
But the freedom from authority that was implicit in widening
democracy led to another surrender. Economic productivity
and the market psychology created a vast economic machine,
dedicated to the worship of goods as ends in themselves, and
controlled by monopolistic factions. Both middle-class and lower-
class man became "cogs" in the machine. The private conscience
was swallowed up in the new "social" self, as mass advertising,
mass propaganda, and irrational political appeals blurred issues,

as well as distinctions between what was significant and what was trivial.

Modern alienated man, says Fromm with an aside to Marx, "does not only sell commodities, he sells himself." His autonomy has all but vanished, his capacity for critical thinking has become dulled, and he feels fearful and insignificant. No wonder Mickey Mouse is a cultural hero: he is the little fellow in an uneven contest with great powers which are always threatening to engulf him. "Whistling in the dark" won't help; either man moves from "negative" to "positive" freedom, Fromm warns, or he is in severe jeopardy, because of his inability to cope with the psychic burden, of surrendering his freedoms altogether.[16]

In *The Neurotic Personality of Our Time*, Karen Horney had described four methods by which the beleagured neurotic might escape from oppressive anxieties and achieve a limited, "secondary," satisfaction. Fromm offers four similar categories, bluntly calling them "mechanisms of escape." All are understandable because no man is immune to their temptations and tendencies —but all have dangerous psychic and social implications. Two of these "mechanisms of escape" are the interlocking faces of authoritarianism, representing attempts to create new "secondary bonds." One is masochistic dependence (parallel to Horney's "neurotic need for affection"); the other is sadistic exploitation (parallel to Horney's "neurotic striving for power"). Then there is "destructiveness," where the goal is not symbiotic union but elimination of all "threats." (Horney had a category of "neurotic withdrawal," which is at least partly related.) Finally, there is "automaton conformity" (similar to Horney's "neurotic submissiveness"), which Fromm describes as "pseudo-spontaneity": what are presumably one's own opinions are unconsciously derived from other, powerful influences. It is nothing less than the total loss of the self. Some of these "escape mechanisms," or variations on them, emerge later, in *Man For Himself*, as full-fledged "character types."

The final portions of *Escape from Freedom* are devoted to a psychological analysis of Nazism and of the alternatives currently facing Western democracies. On Nazism, Fromm builds on his unpublished Frankfurt study and on Harold Lasswell's study of the German middle class. Negativism and resignation, Fromm concludes, characterized German working-class attitudes in the 1930's. But the lower-middle class, faced by the unforgettable memory of crushing military defeat, the loss of monarchic stability, and the economic decline after World War I, greeted Nazism with enthusiasm.

Fromm points to Hitler and Goebbels as perfect demonstrations of the "authoritarian character," who, like Luther and Calvin, inculcated a "systematized ideology" into the readily victimized masses. While preaching self-sacrifice, the Nazis reveled in power over their "contemptible" flock. And the symbiotic nature of their characters, Fromm says, was clear: they behaved sadistically toward inferiors, and they submitted masochistically to the "higher powers." In the next few years, Fromm wrote a few more short pieces on Nazism, but he added nothing essential to his analysis.[17]

As for Western democracy, Fromm feels Americans need "thoughts of our own" in a culture that, through myriad social pressures and a basically "anonymous authority," stresses conformity at any cost. The freest men, he says, are those for whom no artificial barriers exist between "self" and "activity." The democratic goal must be "growth and expansion" of the individual, concurrently established as the goal for society itself. This necessitates a planned economy, he is sure, with a balance between centralized and decentralized authority. Fromm only sketches these notions here, pointing toward future books for elaboration. In a review of *Escape from Freedom*, anthropologist Ashley Montagu remarked presciently that it would always contain "the essence of the author's considered conclusions."

In one stroke, the book established Fromm's reputation as one of the most provocative thinkers of his time, and it has gone through twenty-six reprintings in thirty years. Many reviewers greeted it enthusiastically, Dwight MacDonald, for example, calling it a "book of the greatest importance." It was heralded by others as a "must" work for clinical psychologists, and as a sign that social psychology finally was "coming of age." Sullivan's journal, *Psychiatry*, devoted eight separate reviews and twenty-five pages to *Escape from Freedom*. Sullivanite Patrick Mullahy thought that Fromm had underrated the impact of science in the modern world, but his over-all estimate was highly favorable. He was most impressed by Fromm's philosophical and moral contributions to "the cause of freedom."

Unsurprisingly, some scholars reviewing the book took issue

with Fromm on matters basic to their own perspectives. Psychoanalyst Karl Menninger took a classically Freudian position by finding Fromm "wholly within his rights in applying psychoanalytic theory to sociological problems," but demurred at the use of social science to modify orthodox psychoanalysis. Fromm, charged Menninger, was a mere "lay analyst" who was "presumptuous" to criticize Freud so sharply. And he raised a charge that was to be echoed many times in ensuing years: Fromm rarely quoted or cited psychoanalysts, and he had failed to furnish "empirical and experimental" evidence.[18]

One reviewer asserted that he had "a violent quarrel" with Fromm because religion ought to be "placed more centrally in any analysis of ultimate concerns." At an opposite pole, a reviewer who was unconcerned about the absence of "higher powers" in Fromm's analysis felt instead that he had "undervalued biology." In later years, Fromm would pay great attention to religion—so much so, in fact, that some of his chief admirers would include prominent theologians. Fromm has never, however, really dealt with the point about "undervaluing" biology. In one passage, he remarks that genetics is a "given," and that psychoanalysis is concerned only with life experience. Obviously, psychosomatic theorists like Franz Alexander would disagree strongly.

Some critics also charged that Fromm oversimplified history; that his approach to the Reformation was lopsided; and that, in characterizing Luther almost exclusively as a "hater," he had created a crude stereotype. Fromm had admitted in *Escape from Freedom* that his historical interpretation was far from complete, and not totally balanced. ("Objectivity," he once remarked, "does not mean 'detachment.'") But he insisted that he was not trying to capture the "full" Luther, nor all of the mechanisms at work in so multiform a phenomenon as the Protestant Reformation. One had to make a choice, he explained: either one could be selective, emphasizing what seemed most crucial, and thus wrestle some basic meaning out of events, or one simply could yield up history to a mass of meaningless data.

Anthropologist Ruth Benedict may have put her finger on the key qualities of the book; while expressing some reservations about Fromm's incursions into her particular specialty, she praised *Escape from Freedom* for the great range of territory it did encompass. His fusion, she said, of social change, educational process, and personal therapy was substantially accurate and extremely important. And equally significant, she continued, was the fact that Fromm had struck precisely the right note in conveying the spirit of his age: "Modern man's feeling of loneliness and insignificance has never been put more frankly in its social context. ... Any society which promotes freedom must reckon also with the psychological havoc it is furthering."[19]

CHAPTER 3

The Nature of Man

I "Self" and the Roots of Morality

NO SINGLE idea in all of Fromm's work has been more elusive and controversial than his conception of the "self." And, since his pivotal book *Escape from Freedom,* none has been more fundamental to his total theory. The "self" becomes the cornerstone of "social character." It becomes Fromm's bridge for connecting science and moral philosophy. It is also the core around which he builds a cautious optimism about human possibilities. Logically, the critics who are unconvinced about Fromm's conception of the self believe, as a consequence, that his whole theoretical structure collapses.

The central line in most twentieth-century cultural anthropology, in behavioristic psychology, and in American social science generally has been deterministic, specifically environmentalist. So much so that the very term "self" has come to seem archaic, a throwback to the discredited metaphysics of an unenlightened age. Since David Hume, insists one political philosopher, the self as a substance has been "exposed ... as the bastard of confused language and fevered imagination," and has never been restored to "philosophical respectability."[1] Unfortunately for those who enjoy keeping neat balance books of the history of ideas and who periodically close out dead accounts, supposedly moribund ideas keep popping up again. In the hands of the so-called Neo-Freudians, as Floyd Matson remarks in *The Broken Image,* the "old-fashioned idea of the self ... has made a remarkable comeback."

In his early writings Fromm leaned heavily toward historical determinism. In 1939, in "Selfishness and Self-Love," his language was still that of traditional individualism, as he spoke merely of "respect for one's own integrity and uniqueness" and "understanding of one's own self." By 1941, in *Escape from Freedom*, Fromm's ambivalence was evident. At one point he spoke of "the social process which creates man"; at another he deemed man "essentially" conditioned by history; at still another, he asserted that "life has an inner dynamism of its own." But social character theory clearly incorporated "basic human needs" as an intrinsic element.

Fromm was injecting, if somewhat tentatively in 1941, the idea of a normative human nature. The uses of such a norm were obvious: it would offer a lever to challenge both the eclectic implications of cultural relativism and the apparent amorality of mechanistic psychology. But equally obvious were the hard questions he had to answer: What was the nature of this "inner dynamic"? What, precisely, were the inherent "needs"? Where and how did they originate? Was intrinsic human nature morally neutral or ethically directed? And, in the face of Positivistic skepticism, what kind of evidence could Fromm furnish that a self, whether "essence" or "dynamism," really existed?

Six years later, Fromm sought to deal systematically with these questions. In 1947, he announced that *Man for Himself* represented a continuation of the theoretical investigation he had begun in *Escape from Freedom*. The threat of Nazism over, he was now trying to formulate an "objective" basis for ethics; to weld this link between dynamic psychology and moral philosophy, he had to define more rigorously just what he meant by man's basic needs and drives. The title *Man for Himself* likely derived from the Talmudic saying, "If I am not for myself, who will be for me?" that Fromm had affixed to *Escape for Freedom*. It also, perhaps by coincidence, was a direct rebuttal of Karl Menninger's *Man Against Himself* (1938), which closed with a "reiteration and reaffirmation of the hypothesis of Freud that man is a creature dominated by an instinct in the direction of death."

Of all Freud's myriad speculations about man, his theory of the "death instinct" was one of the least acceptable to psychoanalytic revisionists (Abram Kardiner has called it "silly"). This theory, that man's ultimate drive is toward regression to a prevital state, Freud advanced cautiously in his disillusionment after World War I; by *The Ego and the Id* in the 1930's, he stated this belief forcibly. Fromm also reacted bitterly to the ubiquitous demonstrations of human brutality, but he could never accept the premise that destructiveness was man's primary motivation. Indeed, Fromm argues in *Man for Himself* that man's primary drive is toward the affirmation of life. "All organisms," he says, "have an inherent tendency to preserve their existence." To this statement he attaches a corollary: "existence and the unfolding of the specific powers of an organism are one and the same." Where Menninger's book discussed suicide for sixty pages (he cited it as the extreme form of man's basic drive toward self-destruction), Fromm dismisses suicide in a brief footnote as "pathological" and irrelevant to his principal thesis. Menninger drew no moral inferences from the phenomenon of suicide; he sought to be purely descriptive and dispassionate. But, for Fromm, the drive to live and to unfold one's powers opens the door to a "scientific" study of ethics. For man, he says, "Virtue is responsibility toward his own existence. Evil constitutes the crippling of man's powers."

Consistent with his evolutionary orientation, Fromm cites a line of philosophical development for the premise that "something... is reacting to environmental influences in ascertainable ways that follow from its properties." Aristotle pioneered in the concept, he says; Spinoza (on an intuitive level) adduced dynamic psychology; John Dewey introduced empirical inquiry; Freud discovered the psychoanalytic method.

Fromm postulates two kinds of dichotomies in human life, "existential" and "historical." In combination, they create man's limitations and his possibilities; they inspire his aspirations, but they also generate his frustrations. "Existential dichotomies" (not, he points out, "existentialist" in Jean-Paul Sartre's sense of the term) refer to the fundamental conditions of life—and death. Man is "part of nature, subject to her physical laws and unable to change them, yet he transcends the rest of nature. He is [by virtue of self-awareness, reason and imagination] set apart while being a part; he is homeless, yet chained to the home he shares with all creatures. Cast into this world at an accidental place and time, he is forced out of it, again accidentally. Being aware of himself, he realizes his powerlessness and the limitations of his existence."[2]

Thus, reason is noble, but it can lead to discontent. Man's unique ability to create symbolic abstractions about himself and his destiny (as philosophers Ernst Cassirer and Suzanne Langer also have argued but with differing emphases) marks off his

distinctions from the rest of nature. Of all nature's creatures, says
Fromm, man alone knows he must die; and he also knows that,
"while every human being is the bearer of all human potentialities, the short span of his life does not permit their full realization even under the most favorable circumstances." Furthermore,
while man is always alone, unique, he cannot be happy unless
he feels related to others—those who are alive, those who
preceded him, and others who will one day succeed him. Man
is indeed an anomaly, "the freak of the universe."

Otto Rank's birth trauma theory, which Fromm had begun
to transform in his first article, "The Sabbath," had asserted
that man seeks a restoration of his embryonic equilibrium.
Fromm argues, in *Man for Himself*, that man's reason enables
him to know there is no return to yesterday's natural harmony;
there is only tomorrow, where, through the exercise of that
same reason, man might become "the master of nature, and of
himself." For the first time, Fromm now hints at themes that
become more powerful in his later work: the limitations of
reason, and the belief that the path of evolution leads to the
possibility of "transcendence."

Fromm sees existential dichotomies (there are others aside
from the basic life-death dichotomy) as, by definition, insuperable. But the contradictions he calls "historical dichotomies"
are not. Cultural lags, technological gaps, and all the other
discrepancies between what man might achieve and what he
does achieve are potentially remediable. Within the limits
imposed by his culture, man can do much. Like John Locke and
the *philosophes* of the eighteenth century, Fromm exhorts man
to devote his energies toward understanding and improving
the real world. "There is no meaning to life," says Fromm,
"except the meaning man gives his life by the unfolding of his
powers, by living productively."[3]

Passages like this one, which seem to partake almost equally
of rationalism, naturalism, and mysticism, have led Edgar Friedenberg in "Neo-Freudianism and Erich Fromm," to comment
that the texture of Fromm's thought is perhaps closer to that
of Martin Buber than to that of Freud. A few parallels between
Fromm and Buber have already been noted; the matter might be
pursued a little farther. Like Fromm, Buber, a much older man,
came from a rabbinical family and read widely in Jewish mysticism. He too studied the Meister Eckhart of whom Fromm always

had been so fond; and, although the mystical tendencies of Buber's mind went deeper than Fromm's, his variety of mysticism has also been characterized as "mild" and certainly as nonascetic in orientation.

For Buber, the pursuit of man's "wholeness" was also a fundamental aim; he spoke continually of the necessity of establishing "genuine" (Fromm's word is "authentic") relations with other people and with the surrounding environment. Buber's concept of self had a theological base while Fromm's has not, but Buber's "self" was also not a concrete essence. Rather, it was a fusion of man's deepest nature with all other aspects of life—especially one's fellow man. Both men also developed interests in Zen Buddhism and communitarian Socialism. Since 1941, Fromm has maintained that "relatedness is the key problem of psychology" and that it is bound up with yearnings and frustrations. Buber could write in 1913 in *I and Thou*, "The development of the soul in the child is inextricably bound up with that of the longing for the *Thou*, with the satisfaction and the disappointment of his longing, with the game of his experiments and the tragic seriousness of his perplexity." There is no direct reference by Fromm to Buber in *Escape from Freedom* or in *Man for Himself* (although there are some brief ones in later books). But a most interesting coincidence in terminology occurs in *Escape from Freedom* when Fromm speaks of family hostilities as "sharpening the distinction between the 'I' and the 'thou.'"

Buber would seem to have had one great advantage, epistemologically speaking. Like Paul Tillich but unlike Fromm, he professed a God; and he therefore had a theological "ground" on which to establish his theories of "inner man." One either shared Buber's theistic assumptions or one rejected them. Fromm, despite later additions to his own theory, remains that curious paradox, as he says, an "atheistic mystic." Religious thinkers have often admired Fromm's theory of man, even while they have insisted that a missing link—God—ought to be inserted. Walker Percy, for example, simply cannot make sense out of Fromm's position half inside and half outside of religion. Fromm, he says in *America*, is surely in good company when he centers on the theme of "transcendence." This concept, says Percy, is agreed upon as an "inveterate trait" of man by thinkers as different as Gabriel Marcel and Jean-Paul Sartre: man must indeed "surpass himself." But Percy believes that Fromm uses "transcendence" to mean little more than "creativity," and he finds that a "curious" and overly secular usage.[4]

Positivists have been much more caustic in their criticism, and two examples should indicate something of the nature and range of such critiques. John Schaar, to begin with, is a political philosopher who describes Fromm as a naturalist "in disguise." The disguise, he says, is Fromm's cloak of humanism, but the hidden naturalism is revealed when it turns out that man doesn't create ethical postulates; rather, he "discovers" them in his own nature. Schaar charges Fromm with committing the "naturalistic fallacy" because he doesn't realize that "society is not a mere extension of nature but an independent realm of being which follows its own laws." Furthermore, Fromm's naturalism is seen as a futile effort to define the "good." To do this, argues Schaar, requires that one have a complete knowledge of nature—which Fromm obviously doesn't have. Fromm's final naturalistic sin, says Schaar, is that he admits the existence of "evil." Since Fromm's total frame of reference is "nature," evil must come from nature. But, since naturalism holds that what is natural is good, Fromm is caught in a hopeless self-contradiction.[5]

Whether the contradiction is created by Fromm or is largely the result of the categories that Schaar insists on squeezing him into is an open question. Schaar's arguments are valid given his premises; but "valid" means internally consistent and does not necessarily reflect either the "truth" of Fromm's ideas or even the meaning of Fromm's ideas. Thus, Thomas Aquinas's four "proofs" of God, or Hume's "disproof" of Berkeley's "disproof" of Locke's "disproof" of Medieval logic, or Schaar's "disproof" of Fromm's naturalism, are quite capable of being turned inside out when prior assumptions are challenged. In this instance, the straw man may be Fromm's "naturalism." There are naturalistic beliefs in Fromm, but they constitute only elements, not the totality, of his thought. On no occasion does Fromm argue that everything which is "natural" is "good"—that is an attribute of Schaar's definition.

Schaar also quarrels with Fromm's belief that "the drive to live is inherent in every organism" and with Fromm's purportedly self-evident statement that "existence and the unfolding of the specific powers of an organism are one and the same." Here, indeed, Fromm is on tenuous ground; these are sweeping generalizations, persuasive more as ideals than as "facts." But Fromm does offer qualifications: he grants that "certain conditions" must be present for growth; and, increasingly over the years, he has admitted that a strong destructive drive (he called it a "secondary potential" in 1964) coexists with a life-affirming drive.

Does Fromm have an empirical basis for his argument that an "inherent" drive for life exists? He insists that he does, and that what led him to abandon orthodox Freudian theory and start shaping his own theory was his own clinical experience. He does not cite details, an omission which surely has contributed to the skepticism of many critics. But it is interesting that in recent years a growing number of psychoanalysts have indicated that they share Fromm's "drive-for-life" thesis and that they claim to do so primarily on the basis of a wide range of empirical evidence.[6]

A different critique of Fromm's "existential dichotomies" is offered by Pavlovian Harry Wells. Wells, who speaks as a pure materialist, sees the human being as an "interaction of phylogenetic anatomy and physiology with the ontogenetic participation of man in the surrounding natural and social world." Unlike Schaar, Wells grasps clearly Fromm's dialectical approach; but he reaches different conclusions. Fromm, he says, tried unsuccessfully to "reform" psychoanalysis in the 1930's by injecting a social dimension. When, because of Fromm's monolithic condemnation of existing societies, social additives proved inadequate to explain how rational, productive human beings can come about, he turned to "humanism"—to "essential" qualities and innate needs. But, argues Wells, Fromm's "existential dichotomies" are illusions spun in the air. Lacking any empirical base, they cannot be taken seriously. For Wells, the materialist, Fromm's "existential dichotomies" are really only misunderstood "historical dichotomies." Thus, reclassification solves the problem—by eliminating it.[7]

Again, Wells's sophisticated argument, like that of Schaar, rests on *his* assumptions: in this instance, that a certain kind of demonstrable reality is the total reality. The point need not be labored, for a psychiatrist who possesses a nicely ironic perspective on disputes inside academic psychology has stated it succinctly: "All schools of psychology . . . inevitably begin with a belief about man's essential nature which forms the implicit frame of reference into which their facts and the results of their observations are fitted rather than the reverse, as they would have us believe."[8]

II Character Types

Karl Menninger once criticized Fromm for his practice of giving Freud credit with one hand but then taking it away with the other. This often does seem to be Fromm's practice. In *Man for Himself*, his attempt to formulate a "scientific" theory of ethics based on human needs and norms, Fromm continually returns to Freudian concepts, and consistently "revises" them. The ultimate locus of personality and ethics, says Fromm, is "character"—not abstracted vices and virtues. Freud had reached the same conclusion and had begun the same study as early as 1908. Fromm now builds on Freud's character dynamics and on Freud's conception of character "types." What Fromm adds are social and cultural factors; the resulting characterology, even by the rigorous standards of many hostile critics, is impressive.

"Personality" itself Fromm defines as the totality of all one's individual psychic qualities. One component is temperament, which he defines Hippocratically as one's "mode of reaction." Temperament, which he regards as constitutional and fixed, determines whether one reacts quickly or slowly, strongly or weakly. According to Fromm, it has no ethical implications per se. (On this point, Schaar's demurrer seems well taken: Fromm may be disposing a little too quickly of a rather problematical matter. This instance is one of a number in which he slights the uses of physiological psychology—as the psychosomatic theorists do not.)

The other component of personality, character, is far more complicated. Character, says Fromm, is dynamic; it is acquired from experience; and it determines *what* a person reacts to. Thus, in this breakdown, Goering and Himmler were temperamentally different, a cyclothyme and schizothyme, respectively; but in character both were ambitious sadists—with the obvious ethical implications. Fromm gives Freud credit for the original concept that character is dynamic, "a system of strivings" which underlie, but are not identical with "behavior"; that character traits operate as powerful, often unconscious forces; and that a total organization, and not individual traits, is the crux of what we mean by "character." He follows Freud, too, in stressing the importance of childhood experience. But, like all the cultural revisionists, he also gives considerable weight to the characterological significance of postchildhood experience.

Fromm's major point of theoretical deviation from Freud is his rejection of "mechanistic" libido theory. Freud had spoken of fixed qualities of libido (roughly, energy) that could be directed inward or outward. Alfred Adler and then Karen Horney had substituted the notion of tendencies (with no fixed biological limits) to move toward or away from people. Fromm's concurrence with this later line of thought is clear; he argues that "the fundamental basis of character . . . is in specific kinds of a person's relatedness to the world." The word "world" is very important because his concept of "relatedness" goes beyond the purely human interaction that Horney, and also Sullivan, tended to stress. Fromm, for example, postulates a new polarity: the vital against the non-vital. Relatedness, he says, takes two forms: toward things, which he calls the process of "assimilation," or toward people, which he calls "socialization."

Whether a man tends to love or hate, to compete or cooperate, to favor liberty or oppression, whether he tends to acquire things by taking them or by producing them himself, these patterns of "orientation" express his character. And, as for character itself, Fromm defines it as "the (relatively permanent) form in which human energy is canalized in the process of assimilation and socialization." The use of the term "energy" suggests that in some ways Fromm is still closer in his thinking to Freud than to either Adler or Horney or Sullivan. As for the polarization of "people" and "things," Fromm seems closer to Henri Bergson's vitalistic theories than to any of the traditional formulations of psychoanalytic theory.

Fromm had already, in *Escape from Freedom*, outlined his theoretical and historical analyses of how character is created in interaction with the social process. Now he describes basic character types, pointing out that these are "ideal-types," not examples of actual individuals. Every *real* person is in reality a composite. Here Fromm had a considerable psychoanalytic legacy to draw from, a sampling of which, for comparative purposes, might be indicated first.

Freud's character types were all derived from libido "fixations" during early stages of childhood. Most systematically, he described the "anal" character, whose character traits—obsessive obstinacy, orderliness, and general tendencies to hostility and withdrawal—arose after difficulties with bowel training. Together with disciples Sandor Ferenczi and Karl Abraham, he described three other basically "nonproductive" character types. The "oral receptive," sublimated at the sucking stage, who was cheerful and generous but naïvely and desperately in need of comfort and protection. The "phallic" character, who was overly aggressive; the "urethral," excessively ambitious and outgoing. All four of these types were thus "characters" formed out of arrested psychophysiological development.

Freud's one mature character type, the "genital," was warm, loving, and independent; he could care about and demonstrate care for others. But, given Freud's skeptical view of civilization as it worked its way into the dynamics of human growth, "genital" man was an unrealized—and probably unrealizable—ideal, and as a result Freud paid him only minimal attention. Otto Rank's extension of healthy man, however, was elaborate. Rank divided character types into the normal, the neurotic, and the creative, each with a cluster of values centered around his "will theory." The "normal" character adjusts, conforms, to the will of others. The "neurotic" is unable to adjust or to find a creative alternative. The "creative" man, an artist, or a man who lives "artistically," expresses his own will and makes his own truth. As for Karen Horney's characterology, it was a direct outgrowth of her "neurotic" forms of escape already discussed, just as Fromm's was in part an extension of his own "escape mechanisms."

Fromm's characterology dispensed with libido theory; but, with one exception, his "types" clearly resemble Freud's. As he later said, in Richard Evans's *Dialogue with Erich Fromm,* "they are parallel [to Freud's] in description of the syndrome. They are not parallel in terms of their generic explanations." And although he had sharply attacked Rank's philosophical tenets in his article on "will therapy," one of his own types bears similarities to Rank's idea of the "normal-adjusted character." At this stage of his theorizing, Fromm delineated three "nonproductive" characters: the "exploitative," the "receptive," and the "hoarding." Exploitative man, as one might expect, wants to *take.* He is hostile, manipulative, suspicious, cynical; his traits resemble those of Freud's "phallic" type. Receptive man is passive, often indiscriminately so; and his great need is to be loved. Like Freud's "oral" man, he is fundamentally, and insatiably, a dependent creature. (Freud himself, Fromm says in a later book, *Sigmund Freud's Mission,* was a variation of this character type.) Hoarding man, like Freud's "anal" character, concentrates his energies on *possessing.* Self-isolated, clinging to the past, he is obsessive in his needs for order, punctuality, and cleanliness. He is suspicious of all that is new.

With this characterological catalogue, Fromm is saying that his own observations essentially coincided with Freud's. But he believes that to *account* for the origins of these character types, one has to go beyond biology and into the complicated historical and social arena. What filters down to the child, largely through the family, is a distillation of the available values. For example, Fromm described in *Escape from Freedom* the "advanced stage" of capitalism which, he said, generated a new character type. Fromm calls it the "marketing" character, a product of the modern conditions of "abstract and impersonal demand." A world in which everything is for sale, and has to be "in fashion" and properly packaged, produces the marketing character. The weakening of the family unit means that parental surrogates now often set the pattern: the popular media of the press and the movies offer models, and the young person hastens to oblige and conform. The modern educational system, too, he ventures, is a prime culprit since it is built around acquisitive, supposedly "practical," values. Nowhere does it urge that time and energy be devoted to serious, reflective thought. For "marketing" man, real knowledge of "self" is not even a comprehensible idea. His human relationships inevitably are superficial. Knowledge itself is reduced to an instrument for worldly "success" in crude, manipulative terms.[9]

For a humanist critic, assault on the values of society is far easier to accomplish than is the creation of viable alternatives. Although Fromm did not share Freud's pessimism about *all* civilization, he took such a glum view of *modern* civilization that he found it difficult to locate a positive character, an image of the good man. In fact, several critics have suggested that Fromm's attack on current social values is so thoroughgoing that he ultimately draws a picture of man versus civilization that is as fully polarized as Freud's.[10]

But Fromm could not accept an outlook of futility, as such titles as *Man for Himself* and *The Sane Society* indicate. His approach in 1947 was to begin with Freud's shadowy "genital" man and to transform him. Genital man, Fromm suggests, can be visualized as being "productive" materially and socially as well as sexually. The productive orientation, explains Fromm, "refers to a fundamental attitude, a mode of relatedness in all realms of human experience." As Fromm once had used Freud's psychic dynamics to fill a "gap" in Marx's theory of man, so now he was using Marx's work-and-activity dynamics to fill a "gap" in Freud's theory of man. No wonder Fromm has presented difficulties to orthodox Freudians and Marxians alike.   ,

In earlier writings, Fromm had tentatively referred to the value of "spontaneity." In *Man for Himself*, the caution disappears. Productive man, he says, "enlivens" and "re-creates," through self-generated "spontaneous" activity, his experience of the world. Productiveness extends to the creation of material things, art, systems of thought, and to discovering and building the self and genuine human relationships. To love "productively" means that one cares, that one respects, that one knows one is responsible. And despite the impact of the marketing society, Fromm insists, "Productiveness is an attitude which every human being is capable of, unless he is mentally and emotionally crippled."

For each character orientation, Fromm lists positive and negative traits which represent points on a continuum. Under "exploitative," for instance, there are traits ranging from "captivating" to "seducing," or from "proud" to "conceited." Was there a theoretical problem created by these scales of traits? At a symposium where Fromm was present, a Boston psychiatrist found himself confused by the fact that all the "unproductive" character types were composed of traits that ranged from positive to negative. This range seemed to indicate that an essentially *negative* character could have mostly *positive* traits. The "two kinds of classificatory criteria," he commented, needed clarification. But at least on the record, Fromm never directly replied.[11]

Other theoretical problems have been raised by Fromm's characterology. Cause-and-effect relationships, for example, are not always clear. Patrick Mullahy, a psychoanalyst generally sympathetic to Fromm at this time, raised the question in this form: Fromm, he said, gave character a "primary causal function, and ideas, judgments, and actions are said to be an effect or result of character." But wasn't it the other way around? Mullahy suspected that ideas and judgment were as "efficacious in the constitution of character as anything else."[12] For many contemporary social thinkers, of course, any neat cause-and-effect formulations are hazardous—hence the advent of the concept of "process" and the development of such multicausal approaches as gestaltism, Kurt Lewin's "field theory," or the intricate biosocial theories of man sketched by Harry Stack Sullivan, Franz Alexander, Gardner Murphy, and others. Fromm himself, with his dialectical interplay of existential and historical dichotomies and of "social character" process, demonstrates his own relatedness to these methodological currents. In a later book, *The Heart of Man,* he does outline the interaction between character, ideas, and actions, as being cumulative and reciprocal.

III *Questions of Culture and Morality*

Man for Himself was an extremely ambitious book, even as much so as *Escape for Freedom.* Fromm was trying to work out an original blend of psychic and environmental causality, to insert an element of "natural" volition into a generally deterministic framework, and to find an objective base for ethical theory. To reconcile these seemingly antithetical ideas and methods, he often turned to paradoxical statements (one reviewer of *Escape from Freedom* said he was continually irritated by Fromm's "riddles and anomalies") or to unconventional definitions. "Objectivity," Fromm asserts at one point, "does not mean detachment, it means respect." With this verbal—and psychological—lever, he can examine the implications of "scientific method" in a slightly unorthodox way. He does the same thing with ambiguous words like "faith," "religion," or "self." Quite often, Fromm had sound etymological basis for his definitions: the problem, all too frequently, was that these words have come to have standard, if not exactly fixed, meanings for most readers, and they carry particular connotations.

An example is the word "neurosis," and the way Fromm reassessed it, with implications that were to lead him toward the concepts of "sane" and "insane" societies. Freud did not invent the word (its modern usage stems from the eighteenth century), but he made it world-famous. For Freud, neurosis was the

inevitable result of man's conflict with society; and it clearly
was synonymous with "psychoneurosis"—that is, as dictionaries
still tend to define it, it has to do with *individual* disorders.
Neurosis came about, Freud argued most explicitly in *Civilization and Its Discontents,* because instinctive drives are necessarily thwarted—repressed—by the demands of civilization.
Hence, Freud could refer to the "pathology of civilized communities." All the cultural revisionists took sharp issue with this
rigid polarity and, in varying ways, argued for a more open-
ended and flexible view of human possibilities. A major theme
of Fromm's *Escape from Freedom* was, in fact, the reshaping
of personality in accordance with historical change. But, if
"neurosis" were defined simply as the failure to adapt to the
social situation, did this mean that the man who *did* adapt was
healthy? Horney in particular (but unfairly) had been accused
of counseling just such a survival technique. Otto Rank valued
"creative" men above all others, but he did call conformists
"normal" and "healthy."

Fromm suggested a *social* definition as early as *Escape from
Freedom*: "From a standpoint of human values . . . a society
could be called neurotic in the sense that its members are
crippled in the growth of their personality." One should note
that Fromm's concept is different from Freud's "collective neuroses"—by that expression, Freud implied a *universal* condition
rooted in the nature of man and society. Fromm identified his
own dual perspective unmistakably in 1944, in "Individual and
Social Origins of Neurosis." The ideas he expressed here were
carried over intact to *Man for Himself* three years later. What
any society tried to do, he said, was to preserve its functioning
by implanting its values in each new generation: people had to
acquire the kind of character which made them *want* to act in
the way they *had* to act. This element was, of course, an intrinsic one in his social character theory. But now he stressed the
significance of "innate" human goals. In 1944 he phrased them
suppositionally. If we accept the idea that "freedom" and "spontaneity" are human goals, he said, and if we then discover that
most people do not achieve them, we must assume that their
characters contain a "socially patterned defect." Again he referred
to Spinoza for an early insight: "Greediness, ambition, and so
forth are forms of insanity, although usually one does not think
of them as 'illness.' "

Fromm felt that these characteristics, which once may have been considered rare aberrations, now had become very widespread. In his age, the individual with these characteristics does not feel that he is an outcast because he finds that the same characteristics are shared by a great many others. And, if the individual feels that he may have lost some of his own humanity, he can be comforted by the security of "fitting in" with people like himself.

So there are two categories of maladjusted people. When the individual feels maladjusted from the society, he is "neurotic." When the "defective" patterning itself becomes prevalent, one can speak of a "pathology of normalcy." Theoretically speaking, "adjustment therapy" would seem to make sense for a "neurotic," but it makes no sense at all to speak of an "adjustment" to a fundamentally defective system. Fromm went beyond applying a medical term, "pathological" (or as he said in a later book, "sick"), to social structure and values. In a review of the book *Is Germany Incurable?*, he applied a directly moral judgment, warning against substituting psychoanalytic concepts for valid ethical concepts. To do so, he said, would "weaken the sense for moral values by calling something by a psychiatric term when it should be called plainly evil." While there is no question about Freud's essentially moral outlook, he was never so explicitly valuative as Fromm.[13]

In *Man for Himself,* Fromm supplies a name for his attempt to provide an objective foundation for a theory of morality. He calls it "humanistic ethics," the "applied science of the 'art of living' based upon the theoretical 'science of man.'" In presenting his theory, he raises some of the thorniest questions in philosophy: the nature of conscience, the meaning of pleasure, the innate morality (or immorality, or amorality) of man, and the sources of ethical propositions. Fromm always has been adept, as one writer has remarked, at asking the important questions.

To understand Fromm's answers, it is necessary to briefly recapitulate his premises. Fromm's key premises are that man exists in nature and in history, and that he is both created and self-creating through a complex series of dialectical processes. This human dynamism is neither passive nor blank; it is an active agent, whose best interests lie in the shaping of a true "self." In one sense, this "self" is purely personal, individual.

But, in another sense, its very nature and destiny are linked with all other "selves." There is, therefore, both a private and a public responsibility—linked in essence virtually by definition. Fromm's all-encompassing "natural truth" of life is a nontheological equivalent of the "God" of theologians.

Like Freud, Fromm is almost habitually dualistic in his thinking. Starting from his premises, he argues that familiar concepts each embody a pair of attributes, one life-affirming (and therefore essentially positive and moral) and the other life-thwarting, or life-denying (and therefore essentially negative). On the question of "authority," for instance, Fromm defines two antithetical types. "Rational authority" has its basis in the obvious fact that some people have more experience or wisdom than others and can teach or guide. Its source, he says, is in "competence," its duration is temporary, and its basic condition is mutual respect. "Irrational authority," on the other hand, has its source in power, and its duration has no fixed limits. If mutual respect occurs, it does so more by inadvertence than by intention. Because of Fromm's heavy stress on the "I," on the self, on the growth and significance of self-determination, and on the role of "freedom" as the ultimate value, critics have sometimes interpreted—or misinterpreted—him to mean that he opposes "authority" in any form. The clearest example is John Schaar's book about Fromm; it is significantly titled *Escape from Authority*.

Fromm also bifurcates ethical systems into those which are "authoritarian" and those which are "humanistic." In "authoritarian ethics," values are imposed from the outside; and the interests of the authority, not of the subject, are determinative. Neither reason nor knowledge is the criterion. "Humanistic ethics" rest on the premise that only man himself can shape criteria for good and evil, "the sole criterion of ethical value being man's welfare." Now how, one properly asks, does man *know* what is right and what is wrong? For a religious believer, the source of conscience is clear, and the task of "knowing" is, or seems, easier. But Fromm agrees with the Freudian verdict, that what is customarily called the "conscience" is merely the internalized voice of external authority as implanted by parents or by other social or political parent-surrogates.

Then Fromm cites another conscience, one closer to Emerson's "Self-Reliance" than to anything in Freud. This second, truer, conscience is "humanistic," it is "the voice of our loving care for ourselves." Fromm avers that this true inner voice frequently is muted by the clatter of competing voices. Emerson would have had man look deeply, into the immanence of divinity, but Fromm calls for a search into the unconscious, into dreams. And he cites Franz Kafka's *The Trial* as a literary demonstration of the interweaving of authoritarian and humanistic consciences.

In *The Trial*, Fromm says, a dreamlike, symbolic language is employed to recount outer, concrete events; but it "actually refers to inner experiences." The corrupt, accusative authorities symbolize K.'s rebellious attitude toward authorities; he feels empty, sterile, obsessed with unknown guilts. At the moment of his execution, K. catches a glimpse of his own "unproductiveness," his lack of love, his lack of faith. K. realizes, too late, his obligation to others and to himself.[14] The sources, and perhaps the implications, of this "humanistic" conscience are still elusive in *Man for Himself*. In subsequent books, *The Art of Loving* and *The Forgotten Language*, Fromm resumes the theme and develops it in other contexts.

As for man's "innate" morality, Fromm finds encouragement in the forward direction of history. Man is moving, he believes, toward an affirmation of his integrity and dignity, toward Pelagius over Augustine, toward Jefferson over Hobbes. Man is potentially, *primarily,* good, but the actualization of goodness requires specific "conditions." Evil he classifies as a "secondary" potential, one that tends to emerge coincident with those conditions that thwart growth. Where Freud had argued that neurosis was created by the blocking of sexual energy, Fromm conceives neurosis as the result of man's failure to use his "productive" powers.

Fromm leaves one of the most treacherous questions for last; that is, trying to clarify such terms as "absolute," "relative," and "objective" in relation to ethical propositions. Eternal truth, he says, is beyond man; he can only proceed on the basis of where science stands at the moment: "Scientific knowledge is ... only the optimal truth attainable in a given historical period." And certain problems, arising out of particular historical dichotomies, may not admit of any single "correct answer." But, Fromm argues, there is an objective base to ethics, and that is where connection is made with existential questions. Here he draws a distinction between "universal" and "socially immanent" ethics. The latter arrive out of given social imperatives, such as the injunctions toward courage in a warrior society or toward patience in an agricultural one. These have a temporary "truth" value. But transcending "socially immanent" ethics (which he presumably sees as being mistakenly elevated to ultimates by the cultural relativists) are "universal" ethics: those moral norms whose aim is the "growth and unfolding of man." The ethic "Love thy neighbor as thyself," says Fromm, is objective for all men; the society which is in full harmony with man's existential needs will recognize and instill it as a basic value.

CHAPTER 4

Rediscovering Buried Meanings

I *The Psychodynamics of Belief*

FROM THE late 1920's until the early 1940's, most of Fromm's comments on religion were psychosociological, and they tended to be negative. Church doctrines, he said, were largely promulgated by the ruling classes for their own purposes, or by those who unwittingly served the same purposes. The gratifications of believers served as compensations for thwarted needs. His militant atheism seemed, therefore, in a direct line from Marx and Freud. Hence, with the appearance of such books as *Psychoanalysis and Religion* and *Zen Buddhism and Psychoanalysis,* in which the hostile Marxian and Freudian estimates of religion were turned inside out, it is not surprising that materialistic critics charged him with having "retreated" from realism. Fromm's indictment of contemporary society, according to Harry K. Wells, left him no grounds for optimism; as a result, he sought solace in the tired old concept of the indwelling soul.

Wells's explanation is not adequate; Fromm did not simply switch from devout orthodoxy before 1927 to fervent antireligiousness, and then turn back again to the essential beliefs of his fathers in the late 1940's (pausing only to disguise his revived faith as "humanism"). His interest in religion actually has extended the full length of his career, from "The Sabbath" in 1927 to *You Shall be as Gods* in 1966. To be sure, the religious perspective changed, as Fromm admitted when *The Dogma of Christ* was translated and republished after thirty years. But there is far more continuity in his attitudes than may appear on the surface, and he has remained an atheist ever since 1927.

The real center of Fromm's "religiousness," which is a fusion of naturalistic and mystical beliefs, abetted by what he believes to be scientifically valid psychological findings, has also remained

intact. In his first article, "The Sabbath," he cited the prophetic
concept that man and nature ultimately would be restored to
harmony. The same theme recurs consistently in subsequent
writings, and in *You Shall be as Gods*, he says that the Sabbath
ritual was "a state of union between man and nature and
between man and man." His tone is naturalistic and mystical,
but it is never theological. Quite properly, the psychoanalytic
and philosophical *Art of Loving* has been called the most
"religious" of all his books.

Changes of attitude in Fromm's works have mostly been matters of degree, and reflections of particular preoccupations. Thus,
his work on Zen Buddhism (which prompted some critics to
suggest that Fromm had "given up" trying to deal directly with
social and political issues) was immediately followed by *May
Man Prevail?* which was a solidly documented study of Cold
War psychology and of the political, economic, and military
conditions which had helped produce it.

Specifically, what were Fromm's developing thoughts about
religion in the years before and just after *Man for Himself?*
Even in the 1930's, when "Neo-Freudian" environmentalism was
at its peak, he was not implacably hostile. He met Paul Tillich
in the early 1930's in America, and they jointly organized an
informal seminar on the relationship between psychology,
psychoanalysis, and theology. Late in 1941, under the auspices
of the National Council of Religion in Higher Education, he
addressed an audience that included theologians as well as
social scientists. He argued that something akin to religious
feeling was not only psychologically understandable but also
psychologically imperative. The next year, the paper appeared
in the liberal psychoanalytical journal *Psychiatry,* under the title
"Faith as a Character Trait."

As he had done with the term "authority," and from the same
premises, Fromm dichotomized "faith" into negative and positive forms. "Irrational faith," the kind traditionally synonymous
with religious belief, he regarded as essentially blind, based on
fear, ignorance, or a need to submit. As institutionalized by
church groups it hardly differed from superstition—witness,
he illustrates, the Exodus account where God instills "belief" in
misbehaving Hebrews by having Moses pronounce the sacred
name or by performing miracles. A secular counterpart was
Nazism, the doctrines of which the German people swallowed

whole, largely on the basis of Hitler's "inspirational" ideas and personal charisma.

Against this irrationality Fromm poses "rational faith," a blend of "original thought" and "rational vision" (which is analogous to scientific method). One can have faith in anyone whom one knows deeply and well, or in ideas which are carefully considered and assessed. These examples of "rational faith" do not constitute hard proof of reality, but, Fromm insists, such faith is prerequisite to proof because it implies "recognition of potentialities and the vision of their unfolding." Fromm had not yet at this time worked out his character typologies, but he believed there was an intrinsic relationship between the two kinds of faith and particular character types. Obviously, "rational faith" would be a trait embedded in the "productive character"—the word was already on his mind when he noted that an essential feature of this character type would be "productiveness."

There should be no question about the psychological importance of the concept Fromm was working with. The cliché version of what Fromm calls "irrational faith" is "wishin' will make it so," but psychologists are hardly unaware that strong belief can generate action, which in turn can help to shape events.[1]

Fromm was not unaware of the persistence of semantic problems: "Faith is not a popular concept in today's intellectual climate." Historically, this was understandable but unfortunate. The modern intellectual, says Fromm, having shaken off the shackles of ancient churches and ideologies, now is "rooted in despair" and has turned to pure and purely aimless relativism. This turn, says Fromm, is not rationality at all; rather, he suggests, it is an example of "irrational doubt." Anticipating critics who would argue that he was trying to sneak religion in through the back door, Fromm envisions a future where the "contents" of faith would be increasingly secular and rational. But he also suggested that "sacred and secular are not necessarily contradictory"; and, in so doing, whether by the front or the back, he did open the door that Sigmund Freud had so firmly shut.

In 1950 Fromm published *Psychoanalysis and Religion,* an outgrowth of his 1949 Terry Lectures at Yale University. Carl Jung, who had held the same lectureship back in 1937, had published his own ideas under the title *Psychology and Religion.*

Fromm thus had in the background both Jung, with his reputation as a psychoanalyst with deep religious commitments, and Freud, who has generally been cited as an arch-foe of religion. But Fromm took the position that he was far closer in spirit to Freud than to Jung. At first glance, this position seems absurd. As Gregory Zilboorg writes in "The Changing Concept of Man in Present-Day Psychiatry," "Psychiatry did not fare . . . well until it liberated itself from many theological preoccupations," and Freud was, of course, the chief architect of this "liberation." Yes, agrees Fromm, Freud the rationalist surely believed that illusions must be shed; religion represents both illusion (a replacement for infantile attachments) and an obstacle blocking self-understanding. But, Fromm insists, Freud was deeply attached to the ideals of brotherly love, truth, and freedom. Freud's emphasis on independence and self-awareness, says Fromm, implicitly demonstrates "his own concept of religious experience."

Jung, by contrast, is seen to have gotten religion twisted inside out. In Fromm's interpretation, the Swiss psychoanalyst aligned himself with an authoritarian concept that is hostile to the real growth of man and man's powers. He cites Jung himself: the religious experience "seizes and controls the human subject which is always rather its victim than its creator." Fromm sums up the difference this way: "Freud opposes religion in the name of ethics—an attitude which can be termed 'religious.' On the other hand, Jung reduces religion to a psychological phenomenon and at the same time elevates the unconscious to a religious phenomenon." For Fromm, who never has found William James's pragmatic approach to truth very satisfactory, James anticipated Jung, while Freud was closer in spirit to John Dewey, who "differentiates religion and religious experience."

Fromm's feeling that he has closer kinship to Freud than to Jung on this matter is not, then, altogether preposterous. Philip Rieff remarks in Freud: The Mind of the Moralist that Freud based his hostility to religion on the close identification which had developed between authority and institutionalized religion —precisely Fromm's point. Fromm's own position on religion (which Rieff calls "an influential compromise"), and the reason he can find possibilities of communication between religion and psychoanalysis, is thus partially transparent. In the spirit of many modernists, he finds ethical considerations at the heart of religion. Fromm states that a similar position was held by early Buddhism, Jesus, and Spinoza, as well as by such "secular" thinkers as Socrates and the French revolutionaries who exalted "The Religion of Reason."

But ethics does not constitute the whole of religion. In listing man's existential needs in *Man for Himself,* Fromm had included a "frame of orientation and an object of devotion." This "need," when supplied by a "system of thought and action shared by a group," now becomes Fromm's definition of religion. For verification that the need is general, Fromm merely points vaguely to "the universal occurrence of religion in history," finding "no need . . . to discuss it any further." Many critics, not unreasonably, would shake their heads at this "evidence," and render a Scotch verdict: not proven.

Fromm ingeniously reverses Freud's conception of the connection between neurosis and religion. Whereas Freud had said that neurosis was essentially synonymous with religion, Fromm classifies neurosis as a "private form of religion . . . a regression to primitive forms of religion conflicting with officially recognized patterns of religious thought. He offers several examples of such "regressions": fixation on one's parents is a modern counterpart of ancestor-worship; irrational devotion exhibited toward such symbols as flags and political parties is a modern counterpart of primitive totemism. Religious "cults" have one great advantage over "private" neurosis, he says: the whole crowd belongs to the cult, thereby enabling an individual to feel that he is part of a large, compatible group.

Some of these ideas suggest that Fromm may not be quite so far from Jungian perspectives as he tends to believe. Viktor von Weizsaecker, a psychoanalyst and philosopher who knew both Freud and Jung, writes that for Jung "neurosis was a symptom of the man who loses his support in religion," and that Jung once said that "all neurotics seek the religious." Von Weizsaecker concludes that while Freud "was under the illusion" that psychoanalysis was purely a medical-scientific approach, "Jung had discovered the religious core."[2]

Fromm argues, however, that the key religious distinction is between authoritarian and humanistic conceptions. The Old Testament, he says, is a mixture: authoritarian when it defines sin as rebellion against God's commands, but humanistic when it describes the covenant between God and Abraham. And he finds similarly humanistic Jesus' precept that "the kingdom of God is within you"—which Fromm interprets as meaning that God is primarily a symbol of man's own powers. Whether a man directly affirms "religion" (e.g., Jung) or rejects it (e.g., Freud) is deemed irrelevant. By such reasoning, Fromm concludes that religion is not necessarily a "threat" to psychoanalysis at all. He believes that Freud, like Plato, became a "physician of the soul." The function once ascribed to great philosophers and religious teachers now is the province of the ethical psychoanalysts.

The timing of *Psychoanalysis and Religion* was, in a sense, acute, demonstrating once more the surprising parallelism between Fromm's concerns and contemporary cultural preoccupations. The years immediately following World War II witnessed a considerable number of books, several of them best sellers, discussing the relationship between psychology and religion. Most stressed American anxieties, and offered some systematic "positive" guidance for living. The writers that the general public came to know best were men of the cloth, Catholic Fulton J. Sheen, Jewish Joshua Loth Liebman, and, a little later, Protestant Norman Vincent Peale. When Fromm's writings on religion began to appear, embodying a basically affirmative view of man's possibilities, some critics contemptuously consigned him to the camp of the "preachers" (even Abram Kardiner once applied this term derisively to Fromm). Such a judgment was both superficial and indiscriminate. Even among the three ministers named, there were marked differences: Liebman's *Peace of Mind*, for instance, was a sensitive, intelligent book that demonstrated genuine understanding of Freudian ideas. Sheen was utterly hostile to Freud, but he was difficult to take seriously because his version of Freud was so warped by misreading and misinterpretation. As for Peale's comprehension of formal psychology and psychoanalysis, the mildest adjectives one can employ are "opportunistic," "simplistic," and "confused."[3] The divergence in intellectual depth between Fromm and any of these writers should be obvious to anyone except the most naïve or biased of critics.

To some complicated matters Fromm returned in later writings for greater amplification. In *The Art of Loving* and an essay on Zen Buddhism, he examines with more care the mystical

implications of what he here defined as "the capacity to wonder."
He speaks briefly, also, in *Psychoanalysis and Religion,* of the
"symbolic expression" exemplified by religious ritual, suggesting that there are parallels in the language of myth and of
dreams. Such symbolic language, he said, was largely a "forgotten language," but Freud had helped rediscover its significance, and had furnished tools for deciphering it. Appropriately,
Fromm's very next book was titled *The Forgotten Language.*

II   *Reconstructing Oedipus*

When Sigmund Freud announced enthusiastically to Wilhelm
Fliess that he had "discovered" the meaning of the Oedipal
conflict, he believed he had laid the cornerstone of all psychoanalytic theory. Indeed, agrees his biographer Ernest Jones, this
discovery was Freud's greatest. In his interpretation of the
triangular rivalry among parents and child, Freud was convinced he had found the kernel of all neuroses that plague
mankind. For each person the secret had to be revealed anew
before—if ever—successful therapy could be achieved:

There must be a voice within us which is prepared to acknowledge
the compelling power of fate in the Oedipus [i.e., Sophocles' *Oedipus
Rex*]. . . . And there actually is a motive in the story of King Oedipus
which explains the verdict of this inner voice. His fate moves us
only because it might have been our own, because the oracle laid
upon us before our birth the very curse which rested upon him.
It may be that we were all destined to direct our first sexual impulses
toward our mothers, and our first impulses of hatred and resistance
toward our fathers; our dreams convince us that we were. . . . Like
Oedipus, we live in ignorance of the desires that offend morality, the
desires that nature has forced upon us and after their unveiling we
may well prefer to avert our gaze from the scenes of our childhood.[4]

The Oedipus construct became so central in Freudian theory
and therapy that every subsequent psychoanalyst felt he had
to come to grips with it. He either had to accept it (with Freud's
inferences), to extend it, to revise it, or to reject it. But he could
not simply ignore it. It was a very appropriate title that one
historian of psychoanalysis placed on his book: *Oedipus: Myth
and Complex.*

Each of the Freudian apostates reinterpreted, according to
his own lights and predilections, the drama and the myth from

which it originated. Alfred Adler, for example, with his own socialization-and-power orientation, could not believe that the Oedipus complex was a "fundamental fact"; rather, he described it as "a vicious unnatural result of maternal over-indulgence." Carl Jung agreed that incestuous tendencies could occur in childhood, but he argued that the sexuality of the unconscious was symbolic. Incest tendencies, he said, merged into and were dwarfed by a more significant familial phenomenon: the developing "archetypal" roles of the parents. For Jung, each person had a residue of historical memory, memory that constituted his portion of the "collective unconscious." Otto Rank believed that the total pattern of child-parent relationships had to be considered—from birth on. Karen Horney argued that attitudes of dependency, hostility, and so on, might play a more crucial role than sexual elements in early family conflicts.

Fromm was familiar with all of these theories, but he also had another direct source of influence. From very early in his career, he had been impressed by the "matriarchy" theories of the anthropologist J. J. Bachofen; two of Fromm's articles in the 1930's had indicated his essential agreement with Bachofen, and *Escape from Freedom* had incorporated some "matriarchal" concepts in a discussion of the value shift from Medieval to early capitalist social systems. Bachofen, who had tangled with Oedipal meanings years before Freud, had concluded that Oedipus' possession of his mother, Jocasta, was a mythic version of the transition from matriarchal to patriarchal society. Freud found *Oedipus* significant because of its presumed universality as a human motive: Bachofen found it important because of its presumable insight into the historical process.

For years, Fromm had tentatively proposed a bridge between these two emphases. He had often praised Freud's Oedipal theories as a major breakthrough in psychoanalytic thought; but, since the late 1930's he also had suggested that Freud exaggerated the significance of the sexual elements. By the late 1940's, he was ready to offer his own interpretation. Its first appearance in print was in 1948, in a volume of studies, *The Family: Its Function and Destiny*. A similar version appeared a little later in *Scientific American*. The full interpretation was incorporated into Fromm's book *The Forgotten Language* in 1951.

If, as Freud argued, the element of erotic attraction was

fundamental, why is it never directly mentioned in the play? And why should the noble Oedipus, the benefactor of Thebes, be "described as having committed the crime most horrible in the eyes of his contemporaries?" The incest theme does not seem adequate to carry the moral burden of the play. Fromm's hypothesis is that the myth primarily symbolizes "the rebellion of the son against the authority of the father in the patriarchal family." The son-mother marriage becomes only a subsidiary element reflecting the privileges accorded the new conqueror.

Fromm's new "evidence" is of two kinds, literary and historical. First, he stresses that Sophocles' *Oedipus* was not a single play but a trilogy, and that this fact matters. He knows that scholars question whether the plays were written in chronological sequence, but he believes nevertheless that *Oedipus at Colonus* and *Antigone*, which deal with later events than the more famous *Oedipus Rex*, ought to be examined also. Father-son conflicts are crucial in both the other plays. In *Oedipus at Colonus*, Oedipus quarrels with, and condemns, both his sons, Eteocles and Polyneices. In *Antigone*, Haemon quarrels with his rigid father Creon and, after unsuccessfully attempting patricide, kills himself. In *Oedipus Rex*, of course, Oedipus unknowingly kills his own father, Laius, who had intended infanticide in the first place. The incest theme is subdued here; in the other two plays it is totally absent.

The basic source of conflict that runs through all three tragedies is the struggle against parental authority, most clearly exemplified in Haemon's revolt against the authoritarian Creon. This conflict, says Fromm, hearkening back to Bachofen's 1861 analysis, is a dramatic crystallization of the ancient struggle between patriarchal and matriarchal social systems: Oedipus, Haemon, and Antigone all represent the spirit of the latter (but historically earlier) system. So now history, or at least an anthropological reconstruction of it, is adduced. Bachofen had asserted that crucial social and moral principles were involved in the struggle: "Matriarchal culture is characterized by the emphasis on ties of blood, ties to the soil, and a passive acceptance of all natural phenomena. Patriarchal society, in contrast, is characterized by respect for man-made law, by a predominance of rational thought, and by man's effort to change natural phenomena."[5]

The ideal of obedience to authority thus succeeded the ideal of equality; order, rather than love, became the foundation stone of society. One guesses that Fromm would find matriarchal culture inherently preferable from the humanitarian point of view. But Fromm is too much of a dialectical evolutionist to believe that historically later developments can be *all* bad. In *Escape from Freedom,* in discussing the transition from the Medieval (largely matriarchal) society to the Renaissance and Reformation (largely patriarchal) periods, and also in a more general way, in an article, "Man-Woman," Fromm suggests that a blend of the two social orientations seems best. Love *and* rationalism, passivity *and* activity, are all necessary for Fromm's sane society. In the 1970's, Fromm has examined the question again, as he has so many others, in the light of recent history, and finds a return toward matriarchal principles, but in a form that he believes "regressive."

As for the riddle of the Sphinx in *Oedipus Rex,* Fromm argues that its importance is implied by the Sphinx: "He who knows that the most important answer man can give to the most difficult question with which he is confronted is that man himself can save mankind." So Fromm finds the humanistic principle embodied in the person of Oedipus, just as it is asserted by Antigone and Haemon. Sophocles, says Fromm, who espoused the pre-Olympian virtues of love, equality, and justice, was opposing authoritarianism and "moral opportunism," which in the trilogy is personified most vigorously by Creon.

Just as Freud and Jung, therefore, found in the Classical myth-and-drama a parable for the secret heart of man, so too does Fromm, according to his own evidence and beliefs. His interpretation, as one might expect, has been accepted with no more finality than those of his predecessors. Freud, of course, has acquired something resembling first patent rights, at least insofar as psychoanalytic interpretations are concerned. But Freud's pristine version of the "meaning" of Oedipus is now widely viewed, despite its esthetic, dramatic power, as a construct that *may* have validity for some families in some cultural configurations, and sociologists and cultural anthropologists have quite effectively undermined its pretense to universality. And the psychoanalysts, it might be noted, have not yet finished with either the play or the myth. New interpretations have been offered in recent years, and some of the most imaginative have come from the comparatively new direction of "existential" psychoanalysis.[6]

III   *Symbolic Theory and Humanistic Therapy*

In 1951 Fromm moved with his second wife, Henni, to Mexico
City. Mrs. Fromm was ill, and their physician hoped for cur-
ative powers in the Mexican climate and waters. When the
National University of Mexico offered Fromm the directorship
of a course of training for psychoanalysts at its medical school,
he accepted. Although Henni died in 1952, Fromm stayed in
Mexico, marrying Annis Freeman the following year. He has
continued to spend part of his time in the United States. Since
1951 he has served on the faculty of the William Alanson White
Institute of Psychiatry in New York; and in recent years he has
also been associated with New York University and the New
School of Social Research. From 1957 through 1961, he taught
seminars at Michigan State University.

Despite Fromm's various positions in the United States and
Mexico (where he is now director of the Mexican Institute of
Psychoanalysis and professor of psychoanalysis at the medical
school), he continued to write steadily—six books appeared
between 1951 and 1961. The year he went to Mexico, he published *The Forgotten Language,* in which his essay about Oedipus appeared. The focus of the book was symbolic language
seen from a psychoanalytic point of view, with materials based
on lectures he had given at Bennington College.

Symbolic language, he said, possesses its own special logic,
grammar, and syntax; and it is man's only universal language.
It is a language one must grasp because "its understanding
brings us in touch with one of the most significant sources of
wisdom, that of the myth, and it brings us in touch with the
deeper layers of our own personalities." Fromm's general outline
of symbolic theory is not especially original; but, considering
the difficulties of the topic, it is unusually concise and lucid.
Briefly, he discusses three orders of symbols: "conventional,"
"accidental," and "universal." Conventional symbols can be
exemplified by words which stand for familiar objects; their
"meaning" becomes common currency because people share a
particular culture at a particular time. Accidental symbols are
created by individual experience and the connotations which
become attached; they are one's "private" meanings. Universal
symbols develop out of intrinsic relationships between a symbol
and the object or idea which it represents. Fire and water, for

example, "suggest by their very nature certain emotional and
mental experiences" which are in turn symbolized. Of course,
fire and water may generate different connotations in different
civilizations and at different times—these variations Fromm calls
"dialects" of the universal symbolic language.

Fromm's symbolic analysis differs from that of Carl Jung and
some anthropologists in several respects. Jung postulated basic
symbolic constructions, "archetypes," common to all men. At
least some of the time (Jung was ambiguous on this matter) these
"archetypes" supposedly derived from a pan-human "racial
memory." Fromm finds the racial inheritance theory unscientific
and extraneous, as do most social scientists, since the "meanings" of these symbols are accessible to everyone. Additionally,
Fromm stresses the importance of "conventional" symbols,
whereas the well-known cultural anthropologist Joseph Campbell
(*Hero with a Thousand Faces*) minimizes them. The distinction is significant, because "conventional" symbols are the products of history and culture—extremely basic considerations in
Fromm's over-all theory of man.[7]

Aside from Fromm's interpretation of the Oedipus myth, which
has already been discussed, *The Forgotten Language* also contains a brief analysis of the "feminist triumph" in the tale generally known as "Little Red Riding-hood," and a slightly more
extended interpretation of Kafka's *The Trial* than had appeared
in *Psychoanalysis and Religion*. Both pieces are provocative,
and legends and literature are fruitful fields for symbolic investigation. But Fromm's interpretations are too restricted in their
focus; literary exegesis is not his specialty.

The largest section of the book is devoted to dream analysis.
Freud's *Interpretation of Dreams* is a classic of psychoanalysis,
as well as Freud's own favorite among his works. He believed
that dreams reveal our innermost passions and fear; the dream,
he said, is the "royal road to the unconscious." Fromm concurs,
but he differs sharply from Freud, and from Jung, on the nature
of the "self" revealed in dreams and on what it can tell the
dreamer.

Freud had assumed that man's basic strivings are repressed
by a powerful "censor," in the form of neurotic symptoms. But
during sleep, he said, the censor is weakened; and one's strivings, especially prohibited sexual desires, leap to life in dreams.
Since, for Freud, all the irrational urges are rooted in childhood

fantasies and frustrations connected with the Oedipal triangle, most symbols are sexual; and the dreaming adult is in reality the child reasserting itself. As for Jung, his interpretations of dreams hinge on his belief that there is a "source of revelation transcending us." The dream thus becomes an impersonal event, a fount of external wisdom and truth. For Freud, dreams are largely the distorted imagery of primitive sexual urges; for Jung, dreams are a symbolic panorama of Jungian religious concepts.

Fromm believes that dreams are more personal than Jung believed and not necessarily so irrational as Freud believed. The dream state is ambivalent, Fromm says: "We are not only less reasonable and less decent in our dreams but . . . we are also more intelligent, wiser, and capable of better judgment." Rejecting both Plato's idealism and Freud's hostile view of civilization, Fromm argues that culture can be either beneficial or detrimental; cultural impact on man's total emotional condition can go in any of several directions. In sleep, "the lack of contact with culture makes for the appearance both of our worst and of our best." But one decides whether a dream expresses irrational passions or the voice of reason through "external data." When one knows who the dreamer is, the kind of man he is, the quality of his insights into his own abilities and aspirations, and his mood on falling asleep, one can often find out much about the "reality" behind the dream.

Fromm devotes a substantial chapter of *The Forgotten Language* to his own method of dream interpretation, coupling dream material with hypothetical dialogues between analyst and patient. He continually stresses how the dream should be related to the available "external data." Full comprehension of a dream, he says, requires awareness of "the reaction to a significant event which happened before the dream occurred." The analyst's role, Fromm believes, is to prod, to remind, to encourage, and to seek out the relevant threads of memory and feeling that might enable the patient to translate the "manifest," literal, content of the dream into its "latent," concealed, meanings. Fromm's descriptions of how he approaches dream interpretation represent, incidentally, a major departure for him. He has rarely, except in such brief instances as his discussion of Otto Rank's "will therapy," written about his own particular approach to the clinical situation. Even a sympathetic observer, Clara Thompson, who believed Fromm's theories had important implications for psychoanalyst and patient, noted that he had "written very little about the therapeutic process." She wondered, for example, whether Fromm, who was very concerned about the importance of expressing one's convictions, tended to slip into moral condemnation of the patient. "Fromm himself," she said in 1951, in *Psychoanalysis: Evolution and Development*, "feels he has not yet adequately clarified this concept."

Fromm also has rarely offered clinical illustrations of his own. Karl Menninger noted this lack, with asperity, in 1942; psychiatrist J. A. C. Brown commented similarly in 1961: "Fromm makes no reference to any facts observed by himself, quotes no cases, and nowhere describes his own techniques of analysis." To complete the list of related "gaps," Fromm also has been charged with failing to keep up with current psychoanalytical literature; if he does, he gives little indication of it in his own published writings.

The three problems might be examined in reverse order. First, why so few citations to recent psychoanalytical research? His major theoretical source always had been Freud. Occasionally he has cited the theories of Jung; in rarer instances, those of Adler, Reich, Rank, from all of whom he has absorbed ideas. In the 1940's he tended to make brief references to onetime colleagues Karen Horney, Harry Stack Sullivan, Ernest Schachtel. It may be that Fromm feels that his most useful psychoanalytical contribution lies in relating his own ideas to traditional philosophical speculations, to current events, and to the diversified expanding knowledge of the social sciences. He has made it clear enough, from 1955 on, that he considers the main line of psychoanalytic research ossified because of slavish devotion to Freudian orthodoxy. Nevertheless, clinical research in the past twenty years by "existential" psychoanalysts, "humanistic" psychologists, and others could have been adduced to some effect, because a number of conclusions have tended to parallel Fromm's.

Why so few clinical illustrations of his own? Psychoanalysts from Freud on have made this technique a staple of their presentation. Indeed, Freud's "Anna O." and "little Hans" have become almost as well known as characters from literature, and Freud's use of such "real-life" materials brought great vitality to his work. Fromm may have been motivated in part by a sense of urgency and audience. He quite likely feels that the immediate hazards of the human situation demand a wide popular audience and, rightly or wrongly, he has minimized very technical or detailed particulars. Readability always has been a hallmark of his style, and his work probably has been, at least since *Escape from Freedom*, more attractive to the general intellectual audience than to fellow specialists. Sometimes he has referred in an abstract, offhand manner to "psychoanalytic observations" which he cannot furnish "without transcending the scope of this book." Pressed recently on this matter, Fromm stressed another explanation. To refer to real cases, he said, could lead to a dangerous invasion of privacy. Even with the names disguised, it would be difficult to relate what patients said and did in any detail without trespassing on their anonymity.

In regard to both citation and illustration, Fromm may have committed a tactical error—at least insofar as many readers have been concerned. He seems to sense this fact, and, he says, in his projected comprehensive study of psychoanalytic theory and therapy, he will indeed be furnishing a considerable amount of direct documentation.

Finally, what about his own therapeutic techniques? Freud had postulated three methods for unlocking the unconscious: through dream interpretation, through "free association," and through the mechanism of "transference." In *The Forgotten Language,* Fromm delineated some of the techniques he employed in dream interpretation. In a paper presented to colleagues in 1954, he offered his views on "free association." And in Richard Evans's *Dialogue with Erich Fromm,* in 1966, he spoke about his attitudes toward "transference." These discussions in no way compare with the substantial writings about technique of most other psychoanalytic authors, but they do add up to some reasonably clear insights into what Fromm does in the therapeutic situation.

The Freudian method of "free association" was an attempt to uncover buried feelings by having the patient voice any ideas or sentiments that occurred to him. The patient, if he felt like it, was free to ignore conventional forms of expression, or propriety, or logical sequence, or any of the other restrictions that social awareness places on free utterance. In a sense, says Fromm, Freud was counseling: "Go ahead—free associate." This promising idea, says Fromm, too often deteriorated into an empty ritual. Spontaneous association (as imitators of James Joyce and Gertrude Stein have discovered) frequently ends up as meaningless clatter or nothing more than a "friendly dialogue." But Fromm believes that the heart of the method is still valuable, and to salvage its usefulness he proposes various prompting, controlling devices. "Tell me what is in your mind *right now*," the psychoanalyst might say, thus creating a sense of urgency. Or he might pinpoint a subject: "What comes to your mind about your father?" Or he might supply a hypothetical situation and ask the patient to relate whatever comes into his mind.

Fromm also cites some methods developed by Augusta Slesinger. For example, the patient would be told to keep his mind a blank, perhaps by visualizing an empty movie screen. Then, at the analyst's sudden cue of "Now!," the patient would begin to talk. The idea, of course, is to create a short period of total concentration, bypassing conventional thought processes. By the use of such devices, says Fromm, the analyst can nudge the patient toward self-awareness without in any way interfering with real freedom of expression. But more than that, Fromm believes the analyst should himself become *involved*. On this issue Fromm, like Horney and Sullivan, is following in the path pioneered by Sandor Ferenczi. Freud had insisted that the only posture for the analyst was detachment; Ferenczi experimented with transforming the analytic role into one of genuine sympathy for the patient. Therapist and client were not merely to enact parts during the clinical sessions—they were to be themselves, two human beings who cared.

The analyst's role, says Fromm, should be what Sullivan had called "participant observer." Of course, the analyst functions as teacher and guide, but he ought also to keep developing his own imagination and to grasp emotion from the inside. "We are all crazy," says Fromm; "we are all neurotic, we are all children, and the difference between us is only of degree. But unless we can mobilize in ourselves the very same irrational fantasy which exists in patients, we certainly cannot understand them."[8] Over the years, many analysts have edged away from what Fromm calls the "neutral, distant" attitude toward patients, just as the stereotyped couch has become an optional, or totally dispensable, fixture in their offices. But probably few analysts have gone as far as Fromm recommends. As Martin Birnbach asks in *Neo-Freudian Social Philosophy*, "Is the aim to be psychic rehabilitation or an interpersonal union?" This is hyperbole to be sure, but most analysts surely would hesitate at "mobilizing" such "fantasies" during office hours.

Specifically, Fromm is alluding here to what Freud had called "transference," the third technique for self-revelation of the unconscious. Freud meant that the patient, in the course of analysis, "transferred" feelings about his parents onto the person of the analyst. One psychoanalytic glossary describes transference as "distorted perception of the present in terms of the past." In response to questions raised in Richard Evans' "dialogue," Fromm expressed some views about this technique. He accepts the value and importance of this "irrational related-ness," and he offers two extensions. First, he believes it to be a phenomenon that transcends the psychoanalytic situation: similar behavior can be discerned when anyone wants "to be protected by a powerful person" or to "take refuge" in a greatly admired boss, teacher, or minister.

Second, he feels that the analyst-patient relationship ought to be deeper than this single "dependence" phenomenon suggests. Two people are talking, both share, and both can learn. Reciprocation implies that not only transference but also "counter-transference" takes place. "I was trained as an orthodox Freudian analyst," he recalls. "But I became increasingly dissatisfied with what I encountered. . . . I found myself becoming bored." Out of his own clinical experiences and conclusions, Fromm says here and elsewhere, his own theories developed—not the other way around.

About other psychiatric techniques, Fromm has had little to say. Neither drugs nor shock therapy, for example, have ever much interested him. He has never done group therapy, and he admits to a "dislike" of the idea. Deep problems are too personal, and, too often, "the atmosphere of privacy is being continually eroded."

Can therapy save man? Hardly, says Fromm, who believes that radical changes must be made in all spheres of life. But even where therapy doesn't bring major improvements, he is convinced—as not all observers are—that it doesn't do any harm. And in therapeutic activity at its best, "a person gets in touch with himself, with the dissociated personality, and something happens, possible a miracle . . . energy is freed. The total personality has again provided the possibility of reorganizing itself."[9]

CHAPTER 5

Theories of Transformation

I *Alienated Man*

THE THEME of alienation, write the editors of a recent anthology, "runs through the literature and drama of two continents; it can be traced in the content as well as the form of modern art; it preoccupies theologians and philosophers, and to many psychologists and sociologists, it is the central problem of our time."[1] Fromm often had discussed alienation, in his analyses, for example, of millennialist futility among Roman subjects in the first century A.D. and of the psychic collapse of twentieth-century Germany. In 1955, in *The Sane Society*, he took "alienation" as his key to diagnose the "insane society" of his own time.

The "Neo-Freudians," as they shifted from Freud's focus on the instinctual bases of psychic tensions, had stressed the concept of "anxiety." For Sullivan, anxiety was a "whip . . . that hurts more than any of the individual whips of the biological needs," and he sought to chart its path through a net of relationships that subsumed a "self-system" and all the variables in an individual's social "field." Horney moved outside the arena of intimate personal relationships to identify the principal anxiety-breeding mechanism: modern competition. Abram Kardiner, a more systematic student of anthropology, was able to supply a historical, evolutionary framework to explain the disintegration of institutional and, consequently, individual stability.

The core of neurosis that these other revisionists had identified as "anxiety" was absorbed by Fromm into the larger sociological and philosophical category of alienation. His key sources were sociologists Georg Simmel, Max Weber, R. H. Tawney, and most particularly Karl Marx. It was Marx, says Fromm in *The Sane Society*, who "beautifully described . . . the alienating function of money," and who also "gave a profound definition of the bureaucrat." It was also Marx, incidentally, who wrote that "alienated labor separates man from nature and from himself. . . . It degrades all the life of the species and makes some cold and abstract notion of individual life."

Now the question of "social" ills became paramount: could one legitimately apply the pseudopsychiatric term "insanity" to an entire society? Psychiatrist Gregory Zilboorg once opined that such a diagnosis was nonsense: "How could a culture suffer from paranoia, any more than a culture could have pneumonia?" Fromm's position was, of course, rooted in his social character theory. If a society consistently bred pathology in its members, the society itself could be labeled "pathological." A blunter term, and Fromm was not reluctant to be blunt, was "insane."

To make the concept of "socially patterned defects" a feasible one, one needed a standard of measurement, a human "norm" that transcended history and culture. This norm Fromm had hypothesized in his description of "existential needs." Now he presented a more inclusive definition. "Mental health is characterized by the ability to love and to create, by the emergence from incestuous ties to clan and soil, by a sense of identity based on one's EXPERIENCE OF SELF AS THE SUBJECT and agent of one's powers, by the grasp of reality inside and outside of our selves, that is, by the development of objectivity and reason."[2]

Every term in this definition is loaded: Fromm has taken whole books to explain what he means by "love" and "self." Brief comments on two other terms should exemplify what Gerald Sykes means when in *The Hidden Remnant* he refers to Fromm's "deceptively simple" style. "Incest" is used here, as elsewhere in Fromm's writings, in a sense that transcends its common, literal, sexual meaning. He is using the term very much as poet-critic Randall Jarrell does when he says, "The Son is pure liberation from the incestuous, complacent, inveterate evil of established society." By "reason," Fromm means the ability to see the why and how of things, their inner workings and meanings—as distinguished from "intelligence," which he views as manipulative skill. David Hume made a similar distinction between "reason" and "understanding"; Rollo May seems to have grasped Fromm's sense perfectly when he once commented that Fromm's use of the word "reason" really is comparable to a kind of transcendent awareness similar to Spinoza's "ecstatic reason."

Fromm's definition of "mental health" is inherently neutral in the sense that responsibility can lie either with man and his own efforts or with the social circumstances that surround and partially create him. Clearly, though, Fromm is rejecting cultural relativism—which defines mental health as synonymous with successful adjustment to any existing culture. And implicitly the brunt of the burden is placed on society. Fromm, as someone has said, is a doctor who placed society "on the couch" for diagnosis and pronounced the patient very sick indeed.

The "human ethic," Fromm says, the ideal that society and economy existed for man and for the good of individual men, progressively weakened in the nineteenth century. Increasingly, the "market" became established as a self-regulating mechanism and *its* needs determined human relationships. The hub of economic activity under this system is competition, the aim is profit, and neither individual effort nor the social function of a product or process is any way paramount. The results are financial disproportion, an undervaluation of work, a feeling of powerlessness inside an abstract system.

Marx had located the crux of the central human conflict as between labor and capital, but Fromm subsumes this conflict under his vitalistic polarity: the greater conflict is *"between the world of things, and their amassment, and the world of life and its productivity."* The dominant "character type," as we move from the nineteenth century to the twentieth, changes from the "hoarding" orientation, with its drive toward acquisition and possession, to the "marketing" orientation, with its insatiable lust for consumption. Citing Adlai Stevenson's warning that men are in danger of "becoming robots," Fromm insists that "in spite of material prosperity, political and sexual freedom, the world in the middle of the twentieth century is mentally sicker than it was in the nineteenth century. Obviously, evolution is not always progressive.

The basic economic feature of modern capitalism, to Fromm, is "quantification and abstractification." Most people work not for someone but for something. They buy, sell, exchange, and think not in terms of people or of social function but in the literal terms of paper and numbers. Even "belief" has been absorbed into the commodity category, as in the case of Billy Graham's theological hucksterism: "I am selling the greatest product in the world; why shouldn't it be promoted as well as soap?"

As Fromm moves to the subject of alienation, his analysis begins to take on impressive proportions. Sweeping back through history, he finds "alienation" a venerable concept. It is, he says, what the prophets of the Old Testament meant when they denounced "idolatry." "Man spends his energy, his artistic capacities on building an idol, and then he worships this idol, which is nothing but the result of his own human effort.... *The idol represents his own life forces in an alienated form.*" The original monotheistic principle, he declares in an argument which he elaborates on in several subsequent books, had nothing to do with the *number* of gods, but only with the *idea* of God. God was conceived as infinite, indefinable, while man, "created in His likeness," was the "bearer of infinite qualities." But monotheistic religion "regressed into idolatry" by emphasizing authoritarian submissiveness toward external powers: "Every act of submissive worship is an act of alienation and idolatry in this sense."

Incorporating both this meaning of "idolatry" and the Marxian idea of alienation as a condition of man where his "own act becomes to him an alien power, standing over and against him, instead of being ruled by him," Fromm offers an encompassing definition: "By alienation is meant a mode of experience in which the person experiences himself as an alien. He has become, one might say, estranged from himself. He does not experience himself as the center of his world, as the creator of his own acts—but his acts and their consequences have become his masters, whom he obeys, or whom he may even worship. The alienated person is out of touch with himself as he is out of touch with any other person."[3]

The worker is alienated, says Fromm, because he has become "an economic atom that dances to the tune of atomistic management." The manager is alienated because he too deals with impersonal giants of colossal enterprise—with faceless armies of consumers and with a vast, sprawling, governmental apparatus. The owner is alienated because his "paper" ownership has left him with "no responsibility for the enterprise and no concrete relationship to it in any way." Such dehumanized acquisition is matched by dehumanized consumption: one buys for ostentation, prestige, or out of secret fears. Men "drink labels" and consume things "whose whole reality is mainly the fiction the advertising campaign has created." And men live in a world of things of which they are totally ignorant: complicated machines which are "almost as mysterious to us as they would be to a man from a primitive culture."

Fromm relentlessly scrutinizes the whole range of men's activities and beliefs. Men are alienated from one another, through the "commodity" concept of human relationships; and they are also alienated from themselves. They must "fit" into the social system, "invest" themselves with a hope of favorable return, and become a "personality package" on the "personality market." Even the expanded democracy that capitalism helped to create has been illusory because the voter expresses his "will" in the same mindless, manipulated way that he "chooses" commodities. Men have more recreational time, and they use it in ways that are increasingly boring, increasingly passive, and increasingly tension-provoking.

Perhaps, Fromm speculates, the most fundamental loss in men's routinized lives is the "repression of the basic problems of human existence." The aim of life should be to "love it intensely, to be fully born, to be fully awake." Instead, men see life from the perspective of a balance sheet when "failure" in life is visualized as a business failure, then they become bankrupt—and sometimes they "quit." Modern society breeds all of these negative values, and from a humanistic point of view this situation indeed constitutes insanity.

In the course of this massive indictment, Fromm turns directly on his own profession. The traditional function of psychology, he says, from the Delphic Oracle to Freudian psychoanalysis, was to discover the truth. But today "the function of psychiatry, psychology and psychoanalysis threatens to become the tool in the manipulation of men. . . . Their practitioners are evolving into the priests of the new religion of fun, consumption, and selflessness . . . into the spokesmen for the alienated personality." Industrial psychology, to take one of the most blatant examples, treats its central subject—the worker—like "a piece of equipment." What should be discussed is the "*industrial problem of human beings,*' rather than 'the human problem of industry.'"

And Fromm for the first time takes really sharp issue with Harry Stack Sullivan. Ever since their collaboration in the 1930's, Fromm had periodically cited Sullivan for a concept "similar" to his own, or had acknowledged a useful contribution—even while he had noted that their frames of reference were not precisely the same. Now, however, after the posthumous publication of Sullivan's *Interpersonal Theory of Psychiatry* (1953), Fromm concluded that Sullivan himself was victimized by the alienating influences of society. Sullivan, he charged, had taken a symptom of the age and had assumed it to be part of human nature itself: "Sullivan took the fact that the alienated person lacks a feeling of selfhood and experiences himself in terms of a response to the expectation of others, as part of human nature, just as Freud has taken the competitiveness characteristic of the beginning of the century as a natural phenomenon."[4] Once again, Fromm was reasserting the significance of historical awareness, just as he did when he stressed the importance of "conventional symbols" in *The Forgotten Language.* It is one of his key contributions to the bridge between philosophy and social science.

Fromm's criticism of Sullivan isolated him from one of his staunchest admirers, Patrick Mullahy. Mullahy, who had been associated with Sullivan and with Sullivan's magazine *Psychiatry,* had reviewed Fromm very favorably in the past and had praised him highly in his own history of psychoanalytic theory, *Oedipus: Myth and Complex.* Now Mullahy wrote a scathing review, accusing Fromm as more orthodox psychoanalysts had done before, of substituting ethical concepts for valid clinically-derived data.[5] But if *Psychiatry,* as well as *Psychoanalytic Quarterly* and some other professional journals, attacked Fromm's ideas, a strong boost came from another source, *Pastoral Psychology.* "Pastoral psychology" was an outgrowth of increased clerical interest in psychoanalytic theory and practice after World War II. By 1955 the movement, like so many others, had its own organization and book club; and *The Sane Society* was its selection when Paul Tillich wrote a review for the magazine.

Fromm, he said, certainly did demonstrate a "pathology of normalcy"; and Fromm's over-all doctrine of man with existential dilemmas and normative needs was one with which Tillich largely concurred. His principal reservation, as one might expect, was that Fromm's concepts were humanistic but not theistic. For "alienation," Tillich would substitute "estrangement," a concept that transcends all societies and all of man's efforts, embracing a God that for Fromm was only symbolic. "One must ask," Tillich said, "whether man's power of love and reason is *his* in an ultimate sense."[6]

Nevertheless, for Tillich and for most reviewers of *The Sane Society,* Fromm's dissection of contemporary cultural failure was powerful and persuasive. Tillich spoke of his "profound insight." A reviewer in *Dissent* praised "Fromm's mastery in the art of interweaving, juxtaposing and integrating several sciences to build up functional descriptions of collective disease." *The New Statesman and Nation* considered his concept of "social pathology" thoroughly justified. Even his severe critic John Schaar wrote later in *Escape From Authority* that Fromm "is indisputably among the front rank of the analysts and critics of our cultural and moral crisis. He can make serious claim to being the foremost among them."

II *From Social Pathology to Social Therapy*

It almost seemed, from Fromm's devastating criticism of the capitalistic landscape, that he was left with no way out at all. And Fromm admitted that he saw comparatively few signs of hope. But as the title *The Sane Society* indicates, Fromm did want to suggest an alternative, to go beyond a description of what is to a prescription of what ought to be. He is duly cautious, however, about the efficacy of his proposed remedies: his recommendations, he says, are not necessarily "right." But he is certain about several things—first of all, that partial solutions are inadequate. One cannot simply patch things up here and there and expect to convert real sickness into real health. Furthermore, change has to be drastic and pervasive: "Progress can only occur when changes are made simultaneously in the economic, socio-political and cultural spheres." Progress restricted to one sphere, he warns, is destructive to progress in *all* spheres.

This statement seems extraordinary, and Fromm may be overstating the case. As an evolutionary thinker, he had frequently pointed to advances in one sphere or another as history moved along. Two points might be made by way of explanation. The first is a reminder of Frommian dialectics. Each new form of "liberation," he had said in his discussions of history, generated new hazards. (Carl Becker once remarked sadly that men yearn for both liberty and equality, but history shows that a gain on one of these fronts leads automatically to a loss on the other.) The second point is that Fromm felt men had reached a stage of desperation: the "brave new world," replete with weapons of mass destruction that Huxley had never dreamed of, had arrived. Only a radical transformation could make the real difference now.

Thus, as critics have said, Fromm took the leap into utopianism, into the idea of a perfect society. Purely inner renewal (a revitalized spiritual message) which ignores socioeconomic changes, or purely outer panaceas (Marxian Socialism) which ignore fundamental psychic needs, would not suffice. The only feasible cure for social pathology, he is certain, would be to reconstruct society in accordance with basic needs; simultaneously, man, the individual, has to come to grips with his own deepest self. The "outer" and "inner" approaches have to be blended into what Fromm calls "humanistic communitarianism."

Fromm prefaces his own proposals with a discussion of the three basic alternatives that have frequently been proposed: totalitarianism, "supercapitalism," and more or less traditional Marxian Socialism. Totalitarianism, in its Nazi, Fascist, or Stalinist forms, offers "refuge and security" for modern atomized man; but its price is brutal exploitation. By "supercapitalism," Fromm refers to incentive-management or "profit-sharing" schemes like the one proposed by the Lincoln Electric Company. But these still enshrine competition as the god to be worshipped; man's selfishness is assumed to be innate and ineradicable, and such a solution merely converts everyone into petty capitalists.

Socialism, he argues, sees life differently. It has consistently been advocated by theorists who began by believing in human capability and who envisioned a society in which man stands firmly at the center. The principles of most important Socialist theorists of the last two centuries, he says, have been secularized versions of the religious-ethical heritage of modern Western Europe, derivatives of the Age of Reason. He cites the "messianic fervor" of the Marquis de Condorcet; the visions of Charles Fourier ("individualism will combine spontaneously with collectivism"), Pierre Proudhon (we need an "integral revolution in the ideas and in the hearts"), and Prince Kropotkin, who stressed "the inherent tendencies for cooperation and mutual help present in man."

And then there was Marx, who felt that harmony between men and between man and nature was the paramount goal. But Fromm, like Martin Buber, believes that Marx (and Engels too) was too enmeshed with contemporary ideology to clarify his own thinking on the question of political centralization, too sociologically oriented to recognize the psychological significance of the economic factor in men's affairs, too optimistic on the efficacy

of purely economic transformation, and too naïve about the
strength of irrational human passions. Marx neglected the
necessity for a "moral re-orientation," says Fromm, because he
believed too implicitly in the goodness of man—especially of the
proletariat. Marx mistakenly was convinced that "socialization
of the means of production was not only the *necessary,* but also
the *sufficient* condition for the transformation of the capitalist
into a socialist co-operative society."

Clearly, Fromm's own sympathies for the reconstruction of
society gravitate toward communitarian visionaries, to Fourier,
Proudhon, and Robert Owen, to Edward Bellamy (Fromm has
written an introduction to *Looking Backward*), and to a conception at least tangentially related to that of Martin Buber.
Examining much of the same theoretical ground back in 1949,
Buber had written: "So long as Russia has not undergone an
essential inner change—and today we have no means of knowing
when and how that will come to pass—we must designate one
of the two poles of Socialism between which our choice lies,
by the formidable name of 'Moscow.' The other, I would make
bold to call 'Jerusalem.' "[7]

But where Buber's particular organic and religious predilections led him to find the most promising modern paradigm in
the Jewish village commune (the *kvuza*), Fromm is most intrigued by Western European industrial cooperatives. In Fromm's
communitarian Socialism, "every working person would be an
active and responsible participant ... labor would employ
capital." To Marx's brotherhood of work would be conjoined
social and intellectual activities in all their varied forms. The
community would thus fulfill the principles of mental health in
complete outline.

Fromm tries to counter the familiar objections, the whole
Hobbesian procession of human frailties, to socialized, cooperative activity. Is the profit motive, prestige, status, or power the
principal incentive for work? He cites industrial studies to demonstrate that none of these is enough for conscious satisfaction,
or even for a beginning in coping with unconscious needs. Is
man inherently lazy? If one takes a good look, says Fromm, at
childhood activity, one finds that the child never seems sated.
Laziness is a very logical state of mind when people are not
psychologically committed to activities. Isn't the daydreaming of
men who perform "mechanized" tasks a pleasant relief and a

healthy form of relaxation? No, he declares, it is a purely negative "escape" from drudgery.

If, then, there are no "innate" obstacles to a cooperative society, is there a positive example, a model which can be studied? The nineteenth century witnessed the rise and fall of hundreds of miniature utopias, from secluded, ascetic German colonies to the innovative and singularly successful Oneida Community of John Humphrey Noyes in New York State. But Fromm spends no time on dead history; instead, he presents one detailed case in point: the Boimondau watch-case factory in France, one of a number of Western European "Communities of Work."

At Boimondau, the workers inductively drew up a code of "natural ethics," a decalogue which essentially recapitulated the moral injunctions of the Ten Commandments—love, self-respect, faithfulness, human dignity, and the rights of others. In principle and practice, Boimondau encouraged a wide diversity of activities, both inside and outside the work situation. It sought to expand cultural and practical interests and capabilities. Back-to-the-land vacation periods were ordained, so that ties to the soil could be maintained. A political structure was designed that would insure both efficient operation and active participation by members. Human relationships received considerable attention. Small "Neighbor Groups" were established to serve as "leaven" and "lever" at the most intimate level. Both technical and social activities were organized into varied "teams"; social teams, for example, engaged in spiritual, family, health, athletic, and artistic activities.

Boimondau is a provocative experiment, says Fromm, because it has worked seriously to meet the whole range of human needs, because it encourages the integration of varied life activities, and because it counteracts both the overspecialization and the alienation of our time. This community, he concludes, is "one of the most convincing empirical examples of a productive life, and of possibilities which are generally looked upon as fantastic from the standpoint of our present-day life in capitalism."

Boimondau is, if not unique, certainly a rarity. But Fromm sees no reason why co-management and worker-participation plans cannot be achieved, and he cites suggestions from British and Continental Socialists. On a larger scale, one would need to reorganize certain basic elements in the economic structure: to direct production toward the satisfaction of real human needs; to redevise the conception of private property; to socialize some enterprises; to extend the social-security system in fundamental ways. And this early, in 1955, well before some American labor unions and Presidential aspirants took up the idea, Fromm made a good case for a guaranteed annual wage.

"Transformation in all spheres is essential," Fromm had said; and he offers a long list of recommendations. Politically, he proposes a revival of something resembling the old town meetings, where relatively small groups can confront issues and each other directly, buttressed by an impartial organization which would serve as a fact-finding source. Culturally, he feels there is no need to formulate new ideals ("the great teachers of the human race have postulated the norms for sane living"), but we do need a realistic educational system. Such a system would teach and impress these ideals; end the artificial split between "theory" and "practice"; broaden and humanize the entire curriculum; make adult education an instrument for the enlightenment of the whole population. Fromm makes no attempt to spell out details for any aspect of his ideal educational system; but in another context he has written a highly approving essay about the principles and methods of A. S. Neill's Summerhill school.[8]

Art and religion, too, have a place. "Art" would no longer be seen as the exclusive province of élite specialists but would be a basic activity to be enjoyed by all men. Society would have what he calls, for lack of a precise term, "collective art," which would include such "shared forms of expression" as "a Gothic cathedral, a Catholic ritual, an Indian rain dance, a Japanese flower arrangement, a folk dance, community singing." As for religion, he sums up previously expressed attitudes: it would be universalistic, humanistic, ethical, rational, with "new rituals and artistic forms of expression."[9]

Fromm is not sanguine about prospects. Man's current momentum seems to be propelling him toward atomic war, rather than toward social and human reconstruction. The most likely outcome of such a war, he says forcefully, is the "destruction of industrial civilization, and the regression of the world to a primitive agrarian level." A possible alternative is a stalemate between the capitalist and Communist power structures—he finds the two structures proceeding in many ways along parallel lines, developing into remarkably similar managerial societies, and

equally creating inhuman climates of mechanization and alienation.

"In the nineteenth century," says Fromm, "the problem was
that *God is dead;* in the twentieth century the problem is that
man is dead." The only rational alternative, and it must not be
brought about by force, is to become fully human through a
total transformation into humanistic communitarianism. "When
things have truly become [man's] servants rather than his idols,
he will be confronted with the truly human conflicts and problems; he will have to be adventuresome, courageous, imaginative,
capable of suffering and of joy, but his powers will be in the
service of life, and not in the service of death."[10]

The first thing that might be said about Fromm's portrait of a
sane society is that he should be admired for even making an
attempt. In this era, it is far easier to construct an anti-utopia
like that of Huxley's *Brave New World* or Orwell's *1984* or
even Fromm's dissection of the "insane society" than it is to
describe, with any semblance of realism, an ideal world. Next, it
might be remarked that Fromm sometimes does not distinguish
clearly between capitalism and technology. Harry Wells says
that he assaults capitalism so ruthlessly that he leaves himself no
ground at all for reconstruction. Herbert Marcuse, who takes the
opposite position, argues that capitalism is indeed a total failure
and that Fromm is ingenuous when he tries to salvage anything.
Fromm's solutions, Marcuse snorts, consist of "more and better
industrial management," and in so doing Fromm himself is
"partaking of alienation."

Fromm *does* rely heavily on sources like Elton Mayo and
Adolf Berle, who would seem to be rather dubious references
for a total critique of the capitalistic ethos. And he surely is
ingenuous when he cites with approval Benjamin Fairless of
United States Steel about the possibility of that industrial
mammoth's stockholders "buying out" control in the corporation—
recent efforts of that kind with the General Motors Corporation
notwithstanding. Moreover, he refers uncritically to conclusions
about the motivation studies in the famous Western Electric
Hawthorne plant experiment, without indicating awareness that
those conclusions have been challenged many times.

But it should be noted, too, that Fromm's quotations from
Mayo, Berle, and others do not indicate that he agrees completely
or even in large part with the over-all positions of those "re-

formers" of capitalism. He is interested, as he makes very clear
in his forthright condemnation of the methods of "industrial
psychology," in the implications of those studies—above and beyond questions of "morale" or employer-employee relations.
Fromm's tactic here, it seems, is to turn the very data of capitalism against its defenders; he wants to demonstrate how even
inside observers can detect the larger human failures of the
system.

More critics were dubious about Fromm's recommendations
for implementing the sane society. The theological viewpoint was
expressed succinctly by Paul Tillich in *Pastoral Psychology*:
"How can man's alienation be overcome except by a power which
transcends the law and *gives* what the law demands in vain?"
Secularists argued—and Fromm surely is vulnerable here—that
his analysis of what steps must, or might, be taken to bring about
economic and political transformation is so sketchy that it appears
to be little more than a set of hasty afterthoughts. How, in the
face of a massively institutionalized web of political processes,
does one move toward such a radical progression-regression
as, for example, re-created "town meeting" Democracy? Similarly,
Fromm's statement that economic changes of a quite drastic
nature can be accomplished without much difficulty seems to
ignore the naked facts of concentrated power in society—facts
that Fromm, in other contexts, recognizes with great clarity.

Finally, there is the human problem of rebellion. "How,"
asks Tillich, "can the 'dead' man of the 20th century revive himself?" Fromm does not, writes Asa Briggs in *New Statesman and
Nation*, "throw any new light on how robots can revolt." Fromm
himself has confessed, as Thoreau did, that the truly free man is
mighty hard to find. "Humanistic communitarianism" may well
be an answer to many woes, but the road to a sane society is
infinitely more tortuous than Fromm's brief discussion suggests.

III   *The Mystical Union: Sex and Love*

The bricks of the sane society are economics and politics,
but the cement binding them all together is love. To paraphrase
Emerson's "oversoul," Fromm's idea of love is that it comes from
deep within man, and then runs through, between, around, and
over him. It really is an almost transcendental conception that
incorporates both sexual and nonsexual relations, and it merges

imperceptibly into mystical experience. Martin Birnbach writes
that all of the "Neo-Freudians" stressed the significance of love;
perhaps, he says, they even overstressed it. But Fromm argues
it is a measure of Sullivan's alienation, that "interpersonal theory"
ultimately dissolves love into an interlocking set of social "roles."
And a key difference between Kardiner's "basic personality"
theory and his own "social character" theory, he insists, is that
Kardiner's system allows no proper place for love.

Whether or not Fromm is just in these evaluations of others,
there is no question of the powerful erotic orientation in his own
writings. This orientation is not, however, the sexually charged
eroticism of Wilhelm Reich, or the peculiarly ambivalent sexual-
ism of Freudian libido theory. Fromm feels that Reich committed
a fundamental error when he assumed that sexual freedom was
synonymous with human freedom; both Nazism and modern
capitalism have taken steps toward sexual liberation, he points
out, but sexual liberation (as *Brave New World* demonstrates) is
readily transformed by the authoritarian corporate state into a
device for dehumanizing human relationships. And Freud, says
Fromm, really was a "puritan": "we notice in him a Victorian
aversion against sex and pleasure combined with a sad tolerance
for man's weakness in this respect."

Fromm's longest single discussion of sex—in the article "Sex
and Character" of 1943—is largely an attempted rebuttal of
Freud's unimpressive (except to men whose egos badly need
bolstering) notions of female character formation. "Penis-envy,"
Freud asserted in *New Introductory Lectures* (1933), was the
basis of female psychology. The stunning discovery by the woman
that she lacks the key organ "leaves ineradicable traces on her
development and character formation." Her vanity is thus inevitable, Freud continued, because women "are driven to
rate their physical charms more highly as a belated compensation
for their original sexual inferiority."

Freud was echoed in these curious contentions, which had a
presumed validity in the restricted Viennese world of his early
observations, by most of his orthodox followers (including
psychoanalyst Helene Deutsch). But opposition also mounted
early and steadily; even Freud's loyal associate and later bi_r-
grapher, Ernest Jones, expressed doubts in the 1920's. The most
militant and influential naysayer was Karen Horney, who argued
that Freud ignored woman's unique sexual *advantage*: she could

become a mother. This simple biological fact gave women "indisputable superiority" in a highly significant way, and could well lead to pregnancy-envy on the part of males. Perhaps, she remarked wryly, men's assiduous efforts at creative work represented compensation for what *they* lacked. (British psychoanalyst Ian Suttie, who arrived at an identical conclusion, supplied an apt term for such psychic compensation: "Zeus-jealousy.")

Another probable influence on Fromm was Georg Simmel, who had noted what ought to be obvious, that many thinkers (or nonthinkers) tend to equate people-in-general with *male* people—and Freud certainly was guilty of this peculiar synonymy. Finally, a key source for Fromm was matriarchy mythology, as expounded in the writings of J. J. Bachofen and Lewis H. Morgan, about which, as indicated earlier, not only Fromm's first wife, Frieda Fromm-Reichmann, but Fromm himself had written extensively.

Rejecting Freud's conjecture that women were anatomically "inferior," Fromm nevertheless is not very happy with what he terms the "liberal" counterreaction to Freud because, while it presumably redressed the imbalance, he believes that it has gone to the opposite extreme by holding that there are no differences at all. Biological differences between the sexes can help to shape character, says Fromm, but not in ways that Freud believed, not to the extent that Freud believed, and not with the inevitability that Freud believed.

Fromm illustrates with one major example—the way in which character differences can partially derive from the nature of sexual intercourse itself. Man must have an erection and sustain it; thus he must "demonstrate ability," and his failure to do so is manifest. The woman can yield, she can remain passive, she can encourage, she can excite, but she need not "demonstrate" anything in any comparable way. From these biological facts, says Fromm, distinctly male and female anxieties can develop. Man's can relate to ego and prestige, while woman's are rooted in dependency, in the fear of being "left alone," in not being able to "control" events.

The anxious male seeks compensatory assurance in other activities, where strength and intellectuality can be dominant. He becomes a Don Juan, a hunter, a moneymaker. More limited in her alternative outlets, woman seeks reassurance in the kind of vanity which is centered on her need to attract and to be attractive. Social and cultural imperatives and assumptions will either exaggerate or minimize all these tendencies. (Bruno Bettelheim argues in an article, "Growing Up Female," that cultural pressures now increasingly force the girl also to "demonstrate [sexual] ability.") Sexual differences per se, concludes Fromm, can at most "color" one's personality, like "a key in which a melody is written—not . . . the melody itself." Neither vanity nor dependence nor the other allegedly sex-linked characteristics are innately sex-determined. They vary in different individuals, they are neither "good" nor "bad" in themselves, and their principal determinants are social and economic conditioning. There are more significant character differences, he says flatly, between people of the same sex than there are on the basis of sex alone. Finally, none of these sex-derived differences, when they do occur, imply, by any stretch of the imagination, inequality.

Fromm's usual approach to the topic of sex has been to fit it into the larger pattern of human relationships—to view it as one particular form of "love." To be sure, sex can take place outside of love; indeed, for Fromm its doing so is one striking symptom of our generally loveless world. But he insists that sex as a meaningful relationship, as an activity in which human beings are giving of themselves rather than converting themselves into "things," must be understood as deeper experience. This concept Fromm began developing in 1942 in his article "Selfishness and Self-Love." At that time he rejected Freud's quantitative "narcissism," the doctrine that "the more love I turn toward the outside world the less love is left for myself." Quite the opposite, Fromm argued: only as narrow self-interest recedes, can love emerge. As he phrased this idea in 1951 in his article "Man-Woman," "Love is the blending of intense closeness under the condition of complete independence and integrity of two people."

Fromm's *The Art of Loving* appeared in 1956 in a period when love manuals and sex manuals were rapidly flooding the market. But Fromm quickly warned away those who expected "easy instruction in the art of loving." This advice was sound; for the incautious surely were disappointed to open Fromm's pages and find themselves in the company of Maimonides, Lao-tze, and Meister Eckhart. Love, says Fromm, referring back to the existential dichotomies that for fifteen years had been the cornerstone of his ethical philosophy, is intrinsic to life itself. Having transcended purely natural adaptation, gifted and yet cursed by the faculty of reason, man's consciousness of his separateness breeds anxieties and forces him to seek new harmonies. One method is through the intensity and violence of orgiastic experience—but the effect of this is transitory. Another is conformity, where "union" is achieved through sharing ideals and practices with a group of others; but this illusory "escape" achieves fusion at the sacrifice of one's personal identity. Another method is creative activity (such as the Freudian concept of "sublimating" erotic drives into art). This leads to unity, but with material things rather than with people: in an ultimate sense, therefore, it is inadequate.

The desire for interpersonal "fusion" is, Fromm declares, "the most powerful striving" and "the most fundamental passion" in man. In its immature form, it is "symbiotic," as manifested by the masochistic desire to submit and the sadistic desire to dominate. In its mature form, as love, it merges the individual with the "other." But, unlike the Sullivan "self," individuality is not swallowed up; it is retained, together with one's integrity. Mature love is seen as active too, not passive; it consists more of giving than of receiving; and one gives of oneself, not of material things. Who but Fromm would, in America in 1956, turn to Karl Marx for an appropriate quotation at this point? "Every one of your relationships to man and to nature must be a definite expression of your *real, individual life.* . . . If you love without calling forth love, that is, if your love as such does not produce love, if by means of an *expression of life* as a loving person you do not make of yourself *a loved person,* then your love is impotent, a misfortune."[11]

Of Fromm's four "components" of love—care, respect, responsibility, and knowledge—the last needs a brief explanation. Verbal knowledge ("knowledge in thought") is essential, but it alone is not enough: "The only way of full knowledge lies in the *act* of love; this act transcends thought." In part, Fromm means what one ordinarily thinks of as participation, experience. But he goes beyond the instrumental terms of John Dewey; Fromm's perspective glides over into what must be termed "mystical" experience. He goes outside Dewey's frame of discourse, and beyond traditional rationalism, with such ideas as "Only if I know a human being objectively, can I know him in his ultimate essence, in the act of love," or "We are all part of One; we are One." With such statements Fromm parts company with many modern thinkers. For empiricists, Fromm is aiming at the impossible union of two antithetical worlds. "Whatever else one might say about mysticism," writes John Schaar in *Escape From Authority*, "he should not confuse it with a rational enterprise." But Fromm insists that a unified view of man embraces both faculties.

There should be no question about the degree to which Fromm is attracted by mysticism, especially since he has specifically called himself a mystic. His youthful studies in mysticism made a deep impress, and the "God-intoxicated" Spinoza has been a source of numerous insights. Furthermore, in *The Art of Loving* and elsewhere, Meister Eckhart and Rumi, the Moslem poet and mystic, also figure prominently. And it is not just a matter of a "reference" here and there; mystical attitudes permeate Fromm's ideas on many subjects.

In all of his books Fromm has sought to reach laymen; the most treacherous footing for laymen, one suspects, is in Fromm's discussions of love. The love between men and women, Fromm says, has two aspects: "Above the universal, existential need for union rises a more specific, biological one: the desire for union between the masculine and feminine poles." This idea seems akin to the physiological conclusion reached by Freud that each person contains hormones of both sexes, but Fromm pushes it one step farther. Each person, he says, is also bisexual "in a psychological sense": he or she carries "the principle of receiving and of penetrating, of matter and of spirit." For materialist Harry K. Wells, Fromm is merely reviving an archaic theological and romantic theme. But for more sympathetic interpreters, this classical theme is of continuing, and profound, significance. Philip Rieff (*Freud: The Mind of the Moralist*) and Norman O. Brown (*Life Against Death*) both suggest that a similarly mystical current runs all through Freud's own treatment of love and sexuality. If so (it is not always easy to tell because, as Rieff points out, Freud was incurably ambivalent on these matters), then Fromm's perspective is not so far removed from Freud's as one might believe. The blending of sex with mysticism also brings Fromm much closer to Jung than Fromm would like to believe.

Fromm does not pursue the "bisexual" conception into a theory bordering on omnisexuality, as Paul Goodman and others seem to have done. Instead, he accentuates the implications of the polarity

itself into the basis of all creativity. He surely could have quoted
from Walt Whitman's "Song of Myself" on this point, but instead
he turns to Rumi: "As God put desire in man and woman to the
end that the world should be preserved by their union, / So
hath He implanted in every part of existence the desire for
another part."

This doctrine enables Fromm to draw an analogy between love
and religion. The problem of knowing man, of reaching the
"essence" of another person is, for Fromm (as it is for Martin
Buber), "parallel to the religious problem of knowing God."
Hence, by what one might call metaphysical determinism, he
forges a causal chain. The mystical "experience of union with
God," he argues, is not irrational at all; it is, "as Albert Schweitzer
has pointed out, the consequence of rationalism." The analogy
in exclusively human experience is that "the ultimate consequence
of psychology is love." This last quotation alone would seem
to supply a rationale for Fromm's belief that psychoanalytic
therapy should be mutually involving.

Fromm is not quite so abstruse as he sometimes is made out
to be. While he speaks of "capacities" for love, reason, and
judgment, his analysis specifies that one's parents play a significant role in their formation: the "capacities" are not full-blown
qualities inherent in an "indwelling soul." Additionally, he does
not assume "mother-instinct" or "father-instinct" when he speaks
of the ideal forms of parental love. Rather, in describing mother-
love as unconditional affirmation, and father-love as conditional
and as traditionally connected with the property concept, he
points out that he is referring to "ideal types," principles "represented in the "fatherly and motherly person."

Fromm also emphasizes that love is an attitude, an "orientation
of character," and not primarily any particular relationship. His
seminal text for this belief is the biblical injunction, "Love thy
neighbor as thyself"—a concept that Freud, with his narcissism-
libido formula and his skeptical "realism" rejected outright.
"Love thy neighbor," says Fromm, means brotherly love: the love
one holds for any other human being simply because he too is
human. As for erotic love, he says, it has sexual desire as a
component, but it transcends sex. Truly erotic love, as distinguished from the demands of mere passion, assumes "love from
the essence of my being." It goes beyond an emotional state;

it is a "decision, it is a judgment, it is a promise." Thus, presumably, rationalism is restored.

Finally, there is love of God; and Fromm, the atheistic mystic, is far more philosophical than theological as he moves into these murky waters. His evolutionary approach to religion, which probably owes a debt to Meister Eckhart, indicates that man evolved in religious belief from anthropomorphic conceptions of God to adherence to a monotheistic principle. From a despotic, arbitrary "tribal chief," God has evolved into a "loving father" who counsels truth and justice, and then into "the symbol of the principle of unity behind the manifoldness of phenomena." God's "personal characteristics" vanish, and he becomes abstract, nameless, the Endless One. Freud's attack on the idea of God, then, is regarded by Fromm only as a reasonable attack on the "middle stage of belief," on the notion of God as "loving father."

Fromm had said that mysticism was the logical consequence of theology. Now he supplies a missing link in the causal chain: theology logically leads to monotheism, which logically leads to mysticism (the abandonment of "knowledge about God"). He believes, therefore, that both strict monotheists and nontheists like himself have a meeting ground in "ultimate concern." "Ultimate concern" is Paul Tillich's term, but Tillich does not accept Fromm's statement that "the logical consequence of monotheism is mysticism." In a later book, *You Shall Be As Gods*, Fromm slips in a qualification: mysticism, he says, is *a* logical consequence of monotheism. Fromm does explain what he means by "logic" as he uses it here; his explanation is not terribly different from those offered by other writers who have some related perspectives—Norman O. Brown and Abraham Maslow, for example.[12] It is "paradoxical logic," the logic of dialectics which is embedded in the reasoning processes of both Freud and Marx, and which Fromm describes as being as "natural" to Chinese and Indian philosophy as Aristotelian logic is to the West.

Aristotle's logic is based on the "laws" of identity and contradiction (A is A, and A is not non-A). But paradoxical logic assumes that A and non-A do not necessarily exclude each other. Thus could Marx, building on the Hegelian dialectic, speak of socioeconomic systems containing the seed of their own contradictions. Thus could Freud appeal, as Philip Rieff says, "to a dialectical and reconciliatory notion of language (both yes and

no, either and or, true and false)." Thus could Fromm, when
Herbert Marcuse argued in *Eros and Civilization* that love is
impossible in an alienated society, reply that Marcuse had
forgotten his dialectics: "The alienated society already develops
in itself the elements which contradict it."

The heart of paradoxical logic, says Fromm, is the belief that
man "can perceive reality only in contradictions, and one can
never perceive in thought the ultimate reality-unity, the One
itself." Thus, Fromm maintains that the contradictions refer only
to thinking processes, to modes of perceptions; behind these,
he says, there is a *unified* reality. This theory does seem to match
up clearly with Oriental paradox; whether it accurately reflects
the ideas of Marx and Freud is more conjectural. Freud's disciple
Sandor Ferenczi spoke hopefully of the possibility of "instinctual
fusion," but Freud expressed ambivalence about any ultimate
resolution of his "dualisms." As for Marx, the problem hinges,
in part at least, on how thoroughly he rejected his own "idealism,"
a matter Fromm attempted to grapple with in a later book,
Marx's Concept of Man. For now, it should be noted that some
dialecticians who quarrel with Fromm's interpretation take the
position, for example, that "logical laws are reflections in the
human mind of objective, existential laws"—therefore, the "unity"
of nature itself is illusory.[13]

But Fromm finds no contradiction between the "paradox" of
thought and the "unity" of reality. When thought is trapped
in paradox, he says, it must yield to experience. As he interprets
Spinoza, Marx, and Freud, all three moved from the verbal to
the experiential world. Spinoza shifted his focus from the right
belief to the right conduct of life; Marx, from interpretation to
transformation; Freud, from psychoanalytic theory to psychoanalytic therapy. For all three men, says Fromm, self-transformation became the ultimate goal. He cites Meister Eckhart for the
most radical formulation of this idea: "If therefore I am changed
into God and He makes me one with Himself, then, by the living
God, there is no distinction between us."

This paradoxical foundation-stone is the methodological base
of Fromm's personal sense of unity. If details remain problematical, if the analogies are not always persuasive, and if "mystical"
experience continues to be a dubiously vague concept for ration-
alists, Fromm's exposition nevertheless does illuminate his own
attitudes, and it explains why he feels it is possible to blend

apparently antithetical epistemologies. It helps to explain how, as an ex-Talmudic student fascinated by humane prophecy in the Bible, he could find himself drawn to the labyrinthine workings of Marxian dialectics and also to the idealistic philosophers who preceded Marx; to theological communitarians like Buber and Tillich and their own predecessors, the Medieval mystics; to the Freudian concept of the unconscious mind; to such Oriental exotica as Taoism and Zen Buddhism. And steeped in contemporary social psychology, he argues that the principle underlying modern society and the principle underlying love are incompatible. So, he cautions, radical changes in the present social structure must take place; men must create the conditions necessary for the flowering of love.

The Art of Loving is a deeply "religious" book in several senses of that ambiguous word; it is far more intimate than, for example; *Psychoanalysis and Religion,* and several religious thinkers responded to it with warmth. The Reverend Aelred Graham, for instance, said in *Commonweal* that he read the book with "a sense almost of envy, as well as admiration." Perhaps the most insightful observations were made by Rabbi Jakob J. Petuchowski, who found *The Art of Loving* a modern "midrash": a blending of "new insights with ancient wisdom," often directly traceable to biblical texts, and sometimes both distinguished and extremely original. "Midrash" also contains ethical teaching and criticism, the rabbi continues; and *The Art of Loving* is of course steeped in both. Beyond this, the book is seen to fit "perfectly into the traditional Jewish scale of values." A profoundly Jewish book, he feels, it is "moving within the traditionally familiar terms of reference."

But the rabbi is always a rabbi, and he is troubled by Fromm's non-theism. The Endless One concept is fine mysticism, he says; but there are other branches of mysticism, including "other aspects of God" and First Existence. While it is true that Fromm's brand of mysticism has had good precedents in the West, the rabbi finds it closer in temper to Oriental thought. From the Judaic perspective, "if Fromm thinks that he has been able to 'transcend' the God concept, it is only because, as a scientist, he has to take the worm's eye view of evolution: from the bottom up." Furthermore, he admonishes, the Golden Rule not only says "Thou shalt love thy neighbor as thyself," but also "I am the Lord." These latter words, says the rabbi, are "no afterthought."[14]

IV   *The Mystical Union: From Id to Satori*

The phenomenon of "depersonalization," blood (or bloodless)
brother to "alienation," was very much on Fromm's mind during
the 1950's. He believed that Freud had rendered a great service
to the understanding of man by reaffirming the power of man's
reason and by extending its domain even over the shadowy
world of the unconscious. But, simultaneously, Freud had deni-
grated the emotive aspects of man; even while psychoanalytic
techniques could probe "inner man" in a new and dynamic way,
Freudian theory reduced that same "inner man" to a play of
mechanistic, primitively sexual forces. In reaction, Fromm was
continually attracted back to Spinoza who, as Fromm understood
him, had not only "intuited" the unconscious but had also never
lost sight of man's "wholeness." As *The Art of Loving* tried to
make clear, man was an interaction of rationality and affect.

"Man is not a thing," Fromm had declared forcefully in
The Sane Society, and he reiterated that point over and over
in the 1950's. Addressing physicians at Harvard Medical School
in 1957, he warned of the dangers in compartmentalizing human
concerns. Just as, in *The Sane Society*, he had charged that the
very concept of "business ethics" runs counter to the humanitarian ideal, so he now insisted that "medical ethics" must always
be subsumed under, and derive directly from, the ethical norms
of man in general. The patient, he declared, is not merely a
physiological "case," not a collection of symptoms, not a mal-
functioning organ, not a "thing."

Physicians, he argued pointedly, are in a unique position to
perceive the importance of the wholeness of man and to act
upon that awareness. The doctor is an anachronism in that,
unlike most men in this era, he still acts like an "artisan":
doctors "are the ones who see the patient and take the responsibility." Thus, doctors have a greater opportunity than any other
professionals to "help guide us to a new path of humanism, to
a new attitude of understanding of men."[15] At about the same
time as this speech, Fromm published an article in *Saturday
Review*, arguing essentially the same ideas; but he pointed his
finger this time at those who worked in psychology and psychotherapy. Modern psychology, Fromm argued, had, like modern
life in general, become too mechanistic, too cold-bloodedly empirical. Again he warned against contributing to the climate of

alienation, and of the necessity for the therapist to relate himself in a fully "human" way to the patient. This article he bluntly titled with his overriding theme: "Man is Not a Thing." Fromm also elaborated on a concept that he had discussed briefly in *The Art of Loving* and in his address to the Harvard medical faculty: what he felt was the intimate relationship between emotion, mysticism, and experience. His position was in almost direct opposition to the empirical psychologists, who sometimes take the position that accumulation of quantitative data and more precise understanding of the neurological structure of the brain are the only sources of reliable knowledge about man. Fromm insisted that the knowledge that could be gained by psychology was inherently limited. To fully comprehend oneself or others, one must transcend formal techniques, conventional logic, even language. Complete rational knowledge is possible only of "things," and, once more, "man is not a thing."

What then is the legitimate aim of psychology? It is, Fromm argues paradoxically, "*negative*, the removal of distortions and illusions." Man is knowable, but only in the positive sense by the path of love. In "the experience of *union* ... I know ... the only way in which knowledge of that which is alive is possible for man." For theological counterparts of Fromm's formulation, one might compare Gabriel Marcel's *The Mystery of Being* or Martin Buber's *Between Man and Man*. Fromm himself sounds Kierkegaardian when he remarks that "no amount or depth of psychological insight can take the place of the act, the commitment, the jump." In his various sets of logical consequences, he now inserts the term "negative": "Just as mysticism is a logical consequence of negative theology, love is the logical consequence of negative psychology."

Inadvertently, argues Harry Wells, Fromm had brought the futility of psychoanalytic presuppositions full circle. "In essence," says Wells, "all the possible logical inferences from the theory of psychoanalysis have been exhausted. ... There is no further direction in which psychoanalysis can move." There is no evidence that Fromm felt any such sense of bankruptcy in psychoanalysis itself, but there is evidence that he believed it could be enriched by infusions from other sources: from, in particular, the religiophilosophical tradition of both East and West.

This tradition, he felt, had run in two parallel lines, and the basic affinities were clear. He believed, for example, that his

own version of prophetic messianism, about which he had begun
writing in 1927, was quite congenial with the theories of Zen
Buddhism, with which he had come in contact in 1926.
Carl Jung
and Karen Horney, it might be noted, had also been attracted
by Zen. But for some critics who seemed unaware of Fromm's
lifelong involvement with mysticism, his revived interest in Zen
Buddhism in 1960 was a new "flirtation," a participation in a
dilettantish fad that was being popularized by such writers as
Jack Kerouac and J. D. Salinger.

In 1960, Fromm contributed a testimonial to the ninetieth
birthday celebration of Daisetz T. Suzuki, the foremost interpreter of Zen to the West. Zen, said Fromm, certainly could
comprehend the central culminating message of the biblical
prophets: ". . . their idea of the messianic time; peace between
man and man and between man and nature . . . the experience of
true harmony and union . . . the experience of 'at-one-ment' with
the world and within oneself . . . the end of alienation, the return
of man to himself." A few years earlier, Fromm had met Suzuki
at a conference on Zen Buddhism and psychoanalysis organized
by the National University of Mexico. About ten papers had been
presented at this "workshop," including two on Sullivan's theories,
two on Jung's, and one explicating Zen by Suzuki himself. Fromm
had been the boldest of all: he presented a paper which attempted
to draw direct comparisons between Zen and psychoanalysis.
For publication, which came three years after the conference,
Fromm did considerable revision because, he says, he greatly
enlarged and revised his ideas about not only Zen, but also the
theory and goals of psychoanalysis itself.

The book that emerged in 1960 consisted of three articles,
Suzuki's "Lectures on Zen Buddhism," Fromm's comparative
study, and "The Human Situation and Zen Buddhism," by Richard
De Martino—and the last contributor acknowledged debts not
only to Zen theorists but also to Reinhold Niebuhr and Paul
Tillich. Suzuki's "lectures" were largely impressionistic and anec-
dotal, and his audience obviously had difficulty with such abstract and elusive ideas. Listeners submitted a number of specific
questions about Zen's concern for social problems, for emotional
maturity, for the existence of criteria for differentiating between
"genuine" and "hallucinatory" mystical experiences, and for
family, education, and social responsibility.

Suzuki's response was another general lecture, in very much

the same style as his previous ones. All the questioners, he said, had somehow missed the point: "Zen may occasionally appear too enigmatic, cryptic, and full of contradictions, but it is after all a simple discipline and teaching: / To do goods, / To avoid evils,/ To purify one's own heart:/ This is the Buddha-way./ Is this not applicable to all human situations, modern as well as ancient, Western as well as Eastern?"[16]

By contrast, Fromm's essay was his usual closely reasoned effort to make connections point by point, reflecting his customary acuteness at integrating complex ideas. Compared with Suzuki's "lectures," Fromm's orderly, rationalistic approach seems like discourse from another world. Fromm is rightfully concerned about the inhibiting effects of language and about the way that conventional verbalism imprisons and distorts our feelings. But obviously he is not going to undertake, at least in public forums, a different mode of communication. That radical suggestion has been made by psychoanalyst Abraham Maslow, who in *Toward A Psychology of Being* counsels "gradually opening up our journals to papers written in rhapsodic, poetic or free association style. Some communication of some kinds of truth is best done in this way."

Fromm's thoroughly systematic exposition is based on the belief that Zen Buddhism and psychoanalysis, in both their methods and their aspirations, reveal surprising similarities. The differences, he adjudges, are, ultimately, only "superficial." He admits that Freud would have disagreed heartily and would have condemned all such "religious" and "antirational" systems as stages of illusion. But for Fromm, the key elements of psychoanalysis are that it aims beyond therapy, toward "human liberation"; that it seeks not just more knowledge, but "transformation"; that in probing the unconscious and pushing toward experiential awareness, it transcends rationalism; and that it features, following the example of Freud himself, the extraordinarily patient concern of man for man. Psychoanalysis seeks man's well-being, he says; but to see this clearly, one "must transcend the Freudian frame of reference."

Here Fromm recapitulates his theories about the nature of man: the dilemmas man faces because of his ambivalent relation to nature itself, his search to reestablish harmony. Man must undergo continual rebirth: "To live is to be born every minute." Man must fully experience himself and the nature to which he is intimately and irrevocably related. The incomplete man is one who, despite knowledge and worldly success, has not directly confronted the question of existence itself. He merely *"thinks of God, instead of experiencing being God."*

What follows is the most careful explication Fromm has ever made of his version of the "unconscious." Fromm and others sympathetic to psychoanalytic assumptions often have called Freud's "discovery" of the unconscious his greatest single contribution to understanding man. (Behavioral psychologists, of course, insist that Freud merely "invented" it.) Through the theory of the unconscious, Fromm forges his most specific link between psychoanalysis and Zen. Freud, he says, sought *"to make the unconscious conscious . . .* to transform Id into Ego." But Fromm feels that orthodox conceptions have limited the usefulness of this momentous breakthrough. "Consciousness" and "unconsciousness" must be thought of not as geographical entities but as relative states of awareness and unawareness—not as distinct absolutes, but as degrees. (Freud's idea of the "preconscious," incidentally, which refers to ideas on the "edge of awareness," can provide a link in such a process.)

Furthermore, Fromm says both Freud and Jung took "one-sided" views of the unconscious. Freud viewed it as the "seat of irresponsibility"; Jung, as the repository of ultimate wisdom. The truth, says Fromm, is that man's unconscious contains all that is fully human. Both consciousness and unconsciousness (to polarize them artificially) are "primarily" the products of social conditioning. But consciousness, he avers, primarily stems from the illusions propagated by the state's power structure. Such illusions seek "to deny and to rationalize the dichotomy between the goals of humanity and those of any given society." Thus, Fromm concludes, "The content of consciousness is mostly fictional and delusional, and precisely does not represent reality."[17]

These are heady ideas, and Fromm tries to bring them down from rarefied atmosphere into practical application. The reality of the unconscious, he says, has to be brought into consciousness, to *"transform the mere idea of the universality of man into the living experience of this universality."* The role of the analyst in therapy is to help effect this experiential transformation. Here the Ferenczi-Sullivan-Fromm alteration of the analyst's role from neutral observer into "participant" is crucial. Self-awareness comes only when the patient has transcended the "frozen reality" of language, transcended conventional thought and logic, and has moved, through a shared experience with the analyst, into a truer realm of being. The process is mutual: "The analyst analyzes the patient, but the patient also analyzes the analyst, because the analyst, by sharing the unconscious of his patient, cannot help clarifying his own unconscious."

The culmination of Zen is "satori"—enlightenment. This experience, Fromm confesses, he has not achieved. But from the available descriptions and explanations, he feels it is very similar to the ultimate goal of his own "humanistic psychoanalysis," to the full attainment of what he has called the "productive orientation." Zen's goal is like Socrates': "to know thyself." But the method is like that of the mystics: to know from the inside.

Zen and psychoanalysis, Fromm argues, really have many similarities. Both seek freedom for the energies stored within man, energies which have become "cramped and distorted" by circumstances. Both are ethical systems, yet both really pursue characterological transformation. Both seek a full grasp of the world. Where psychoanalysis aims to "make the unconscious conscious," Suzuki "speaks of the Zen-man as being 'in direct communion with the great unconscious.'" Even the nature of the final experience itself is not unrelated: "the authentic psychoanalytic insight is sudden. . . . It starts not in our brain but, to use a Japanese image, in our belly." To Fromm's credit, he does not insist on translating the paradoxical Zen concepts into precise psychoanalytical equivalents—he admits that there are degrees of difference in not one, but dozens of places. As for ultimate experience—"satori"—he says that it may be almost as rare as full psychoanalytical insight. What he does believe, firmly, is that the two systems can learn from each other.

Whether Suzuki believes that Zen can learn anything from psychoanalysis is moot; in his lectures, Suzuki gives no such indication. And, of course, there are other questions and problems— more than one can raise in a short space. Fromm is, for example, almost totally uncritical of Zen; one would expect that his lifelong concern with social, economic, and political responsibility would lead him to considerable doubt about what appear to be essentially egocentric leanings in Zen. Doesn't Suzuki's reference to "The Great Unconscious" sound rather like the Jungian conception that Fromm rejects? And Fromm raises no questions at all about the real applicability of the system for the West—could it, after all, be much more than an exotic fetish for a tiny minority of Westerners, given, as Fromm admits, the almost totally opposite direction of Western thought? And how can it fit into the larger therapeutic and communitarian considerations which Fromm views as matters of such urgency?

A particular puzzle is created by Fromm's comments on authority. He had long since argued for distinguishing between "rational" and "irrational" authority—and he makes the same distinction in the essay here. He refers to the Zen master's "rational authority," which is based on his superior experience and wisdom, and which in some ways is related to the psychoanalytic therapist's "rational authority." Fromm seems to be arguing that man should be mature and self-comprehending, responsible not because he is told to be, or because he thinks he ought to be, but because he feels part of the total human community. At one point Fromm specifically rejects both "irrational authority" and "laissez-faire absence of any authority." These positions seem reasonably clear, but Fromm also says that both psychoanalysis and Zen insist "on independence from *any* kind of authority." Is this carelessness on Fromm's part, does it suggest his attitudes are ambiguous, or are some critics correct in believing (in good Freudian fashion) that Fromm's *real* belief has slipped out? If one were to assume a properly paradoxical stance, one could say that all of these guesses are correct, with each containing a piece of the truth. And one might add that Fromm may really be referring to an ideal, the kind of man who has totally internalized the ethic of a utopian society.

CHAPTER *6*

Freud, Marx, and the Cold War

I *The Freudian Revival*

ONE SYMPTOM of post-World War I disillusion was the weltschmerz of such American intellectuals as T. S. Eliot and the "Lost Generation" novelists, a melancholy spirit that was most lengthily and monolithically displayed in Harold Stearns's symposium of 1922, *Civilization in the United States.* At the end of the decade, just as the Wall Street stock market was about to come tumbling down, Joseph Wood Krutch supplied the final gasp of disillusion. In *The Modern Temper* (1929), with appropriate mock-heroics, Krutch cried out: "Hail, horrors, Hail, / Infernal world! and thou Profoundest hell, / Receive thy new possessor." The years following World War II witnessed a similarly somber mood. Politically, the new mood was characterized by "an end of ideology" according to sociologist Daniel Bell in a book by that title. In more general terms, Floyd Matson in *The Broken Image,* has described the era in this way: "The impulse to action became sicklied over with the recognition of complexity and ambiguity; and the cataleptic stance of brooding withdrawal once more came into fashion."

During the 1920's, the pessimism of Sigmund Freud also deepened: in fact, it contributed to the despair of such writers as Krutch. Freud had opened the decade with a tentative theory of the "death instinct," and he closed it with *Civilization and Its Discontents.* Fittingly, the Cold War years witnessed, as Matson says, "a wholehearted resuscitation of the 'night side' of psychoanalysis," with an emphasis on instinctual fatalism.

One of the first and most forthright of these "Neo-Instinctivists" (as Fromm and others have called them) was Herbert Marcuse, whose *Eros and Civilization* appeared in 1955. In the book's epilogue, which was published first in the Socialist

111

magazine *Dissent,* Marcuse wrote: "Personality and its development are *pre*formed down to the deepest instinctual structure,
and this preformation, the work of accumulated civilization,
makes the diversities and the autonomy of individual 'growth'
secondary phenomena." In Marcuse's viewpoint (which included
a reaffirmation of the "death instinct"), Sullivan, Horney, and
Fromm had all borrowed indiscriminately from the social sciences. In so doing, he said, they had lost sight of the basic
instinct-structure of man, and thus completely misunderstood
the basic human dilemma. Freud's stress on "the fundamental
role of sexuality as a 'productive force'" was radical social
criticism, but Fromm had retreated to a "defunct idealistic
philosophy." How could one practice such values within "the
very conditions which betray them"? Fromm's "affirmation," he
charged, "absorbs the critique."[1]

Although Fromm rarely engaged in debate through the magazines, he had little choice in this instance. He had known
Marcuse since the 1930's, through the International Institute for
Social Research; and he himself was a contributing editor of
Dissent at this time. When he replied in the next issue, he denied
that Freudian theory was radical in its criticism of contemporary
society, and that his own theories were reducible to "adjustment
to present alienated society." According to Fromm, Freud, who
believed that man had an inherent desire for unlimited sexual
satisfaction, "must arrive at a picture of the necessary conflict
between all civilization and mental health and happiness."
Freud's *specific* criticism of modern society, said Fromm, ignored socioeconomic structure; it was limited to denouncing
repressions of sexual drives. As for Freud's theory of instincts
being "radical," Fromm found it, instead, fitting comfortably
into "nineteenth-century bourgeois materialism."

Was he himself preaching "adjustment"? "What Marcuse is
saying here," he argued, "is that any person who has integrity
and is capable of love and happiness, in present-day capitalistic
society, must either become a martyr or insane." He refused to
believe that anyone who sought to understand the meaning and
failure of love in a capitalistic society and who sought to revive
the idea of true love automatically became "a companion to
Rev. Peale." To try to counteract alienation did not mean "preaching adjustment." Fromm called Marcuse a "human nihilist,"
and Marcuse accepted the designation. "Nihilism," he replied

in still another issue of *Dissent,* "as the indictment of human conditions, may be a truly humanist attitude—part of the Great Refusal to play the game, to compromise with the bad 'positive.' "[2]

Marcuse's position actually represented only one branch of the "hard-line" psychoanalytic revival of the Cold War years. Any attempt to sort out the various categories is probably an impossible task, but several scholars have suggested that Marcuse, together with Norman O. Brown, Paul Goodman, Norman Mailer, and others, have more or less transmogrified Freud into the "holy sexuality" of Wilhelm Reich.[3] A larger group of contemporary intellectuals, including some literary scholars, identified themselves as orthodox Freudians. Pointing out that Freud himself was dubious about the efficacy of individual "cure," their interest in therapy generally was negligible or nil; they were intrigued, rather, by the romantic mystery of the id and by the tensions in Freud's "style." And they observed, accurately, that Freud had received a Nobel Prize, not for medicine but for literature.

The literary scholars took an intense pride in their Freudian purism. Stanley Hyman, in "Psychoanalysis and the Climate of Tragedy," probably felt that he was offering the highest praise when he noted that his compatriot, Lionel Trilling, "has been uniquely distinguished among modern literary critics by his defense of Freudian orthodoxy against bowdlerization and revision." Scholars in other fields were not always so impressed by the apologias of literary critics. "Interest in Freud's discoveries and theories," Jacques Maritain has written, "seems to grow greater and more ardent as it extends to less competent groups. Literary men have played an enormous role in the diffusion of Freudianism."[4] The new lay apostles of orthodoxy gave short shrift to the "Neo-Freudians," and here, of course, they stood shoulder to shoulder with psychoanalysts who remained relatively strict Freudians. An important new study, for example, *A History of Psychoanalysis in America,* by Clarence Oberndorf, the former president of the American Psychoanalytical Association, offered brief mentions of Horney, Sullivan, and Thompson, and not a word about Fromm.

Undoubtedly, the major publication about psychoanalysis during these years was Ernest Jones's monumental biography of Freud, which appeared in three volumes from 1953 to 1957, and provided a wealth of detailed information. In 1956, the centenary of Freud's birth, Jones came to America to lead the celebration. Lionel Trilling, who had published an Anniversary Lecture, "Freud and the Crisis of our Culture," now interviewed Jones for television; and he subsequently coedited the one-volume abridgement of the biography of Freud. In conjunction with the centenary, Benjamin Nelson, historian and sociologist, edited a volume of essays, *Freud and the 20th Century*, with contributors from many different disciplines. Nelson was somewhat less than candid in his introduction when he remarked that all of the essayists, "it happens," preferred Freud to any of the many revisionists. With little effort, of course, spokesmen for revision could have been found. What was most striking in Nelson's book, however, was not the lavish praise of Freud, which is not altogether unreasonable considering Freud's extraordinary talents and accomplishments, but the virulence of the attacks on the "revisionists." Editor Nelson himself shared this tone, and suggested something about the mood of the time when he remarked on how different was "the temper of the 1950's from that of the 1930's and 1940's, when formless clichés concerning [Freud's] defects as man and scientist were on every tongue." Will Herberg, a well-known professor of Judaica and historian of religion, contributed an essay in which he took Fromm to task for failure to be religious enough. Fromm, he said, was a brilliant, even profound, social critic. But Fromm was also described as a thinker who had grossly overestimated the role of society and of harmonistic possibilities, tracing all of man's distortions to the "corrupting effects of the culture." If Freud had overstressed biology, said Herberg, he at least had seen that "the trouble lies deep in man," while Fromm, a "Rousseauian," was blind to the "hard wisdom" of original sin.

While Herberg found Fromm possessing some insights to counterbalance (at least partially) his "extreme Pelagianism," literary critic Stanley Hyman had no bouquets, only brickbats. Critic Richard Chase had once attacked the "Neo-Freudians" by making the bizarre observation that Freud had enabled men to differentiate clearly between mind and body (as though the obvious truths of psychosomatic connections were a species of witchcraft). Now Hyman, depicting Freud as a "humble therapist," classified Horney, Fromm, and Sullivan as "faith-healers, inspirational preachers, be-glad-you're neurotic Pollyannas."

Hyman admitted he was not interested in psychoanalysis "as a medical phenomenon," but perversely he was infuriated by the revisionists who denied "genetic and dynamic factors." And how dare they abandon what Freud and Hyman both deemed an absolute truth—the universality of the Oedipus complex?

Hyman was a respected literary scholar; his animus on this subject is so fervent and so all-encompassing that a relatively temperate reader rightfully wonders why. Considering Hyman's paean to orthodoxy, Gerald Sykes may have a point when he says that Fromm's "analysis of 'authoritarian' rigidity may well have provoked certain overemphatic highbrow attacks on him, since the well-worn path of a number of highbrows has gone from one authority to another."[5] However, one other explanation might be offered. Floyd Matson has aptly referred to these super-Freudians as essentially "belletristic" in their approach to these matters (which probably also accounts for Jung's being held in high repute by literary scholars, while the vast majority of scientists and social scientists have long since rejected his psychoanalytic theories). As Hyman's essay title, "Psychoanalysis and the Climate of Tragedy," indicates, he is centrally concerned with literary implications. Freud, says Hyman, "showed us that human life was nasty, brutish, and short. . . . He produced a climate of opinion in which tragedy could again flourish."

There probably is a measure of literary truth in this observation. The revisionists refuse to believe that people are irrevocably locked in libidinal conflicts, that every man is foredoomed to despair by the simple fact that civilization exists, or that every woman must sob her life out in the agony of penis envy. Followers of Horney are not likely to produce books like Ernest Hemingway's *The Sun Also Rises*; they are more likely, as Theodore Rubin of the Karen Horney Clinic has done, to write books like *Lisa and David*. Hyman's response to Rubin's book is not, as far as may be ascertained, on record; but he made his position clear in reviewing Thomas Pynchon's novel *V*. In the course of this absurdist novel, in which Pynchon delivers a powerful indictment against dehumanization of the human spirit, a character insists on the need to love, to care. Such remarks, says Hyman, are only the "slogans of revisionist psychoanalysis."

Not only Hyman but also Richard Chase, Alfred Kazin, and Herbert Marcuse (with his own penchant for such morbid metaphors as "sharpen," "explosive," and "mutilate") are terribly

aggrieved by the "style" of the revisionists. Here the questions
become far more complicated because they involve such thorny
issues as ambiguity, the predilections of the reader, and the
purposes of the author. Freud's linguistic tensions are an important reason why every interpreter reads him a little differently
and why his greatest award was literary rather than medical.
The most elementary acquaintance with the writings of Horney,
Sullivan, and Fromm should indicate why they cannot be lumped
together indiscriminately; only Fromm of this group, for example,
consistently employs paradox even while he is trying to minimize, for the purpose of clear communication, difficult ambigu-
ities. There is much that is important about the modern, all-
embracing concept of "style," but there also are elements of
pretentiousness and "public image" in it, as Christopher Lasch
has pointed out in relation to the late President John F. Kennedy.[6]

II *Fromm on Freud*

Ernest Jones's biography of Freud, appearing in the midst
of so much hostility to "Neo-Freudianism," inevitably drew
comment from Fromm. As Freud's most faithful and unswerving
disciple as well as an important contributor to psychoanalytic
theory in his own right, Jones was in a position to provide much
new documentation about Freud and also about the activities
and vicissitudes of others prominently involved in the stormy
history of psychoanalysis. Most observers agreed that Jones's
book was now the indispensable guide to the Vienna master;
now, as Philip Rieff wrote, the public really could measure "the
magnitude of Freud's personal achievement."

But could Jones, who *was* such a loyal disciple, so devoted to
Freud and at the same time so enmeshed himself in bitter
controversies (he had, for example, been sharply critical of
Karen Horney), really have the last word? Fromm, for one, was
skeptical, especially since so many reviewers praised Jones with
little or no qualification. In an article, "Psychoanalysis—Science
or Party Line?" Fromm charged that Freudianism had become
a "movement." Like religious and political bureaucracies, it had
a hierarchy, membership rules, and a "secret committee" to
guide it. This "party line" spirit, he said, had led Jones to deliver
"grotesque posthumous attacks" on those who disagreed with
Freud—notably Otto Rank and Sandor Ferenczi. In both instances,

says Fromm, Jones's motivation seemed clear enough: the bureaucratic infighting and the personal enmities among those who were close to Freud. Jones "had been intriguing against Rank and suspecting him of disloyalty for many years," and "fantastic rivalries and intrigues between Jones and Ferenczi" had continued for an even longer time.

This pattern, Fromm believes, was symptomatic of what became a "fanatical movement." To explain its genesis, Fromm turns to Freud's own original motivation in Freud's own words: "In my youth I felt an overpowering need to understand something of the riddles of the world in which we live, and perhaps even to contribute to their solution." Now, Fromm in a different context has declared that he himself was motivated by an equally burning ambition. But he argues that Freud early identified himself with conquerors and benefactors of humanity, with men like Hannibal and Moses—identifications that continued all of his life. Originally, Freud had envisioned an International Fraternity for Ethics and Culture. When Jung expressed grave doubts about such an organization, the International Psychoanalytic Movement was founded instead. Fromm believes that Freud still aspired toward cultural-ethical leadership, still wanted to lead man toward salvation through "the conquest of passion by intellect." But "unfortunately," Fromm says, the movement took hold among the urban middle class and intelligentsia. Like Freud, they had lost their faith in radical philosophy and politics, and they adopted psychoanalysis as a substitute. These followers created their own orthodoxy and bureaucracy, and Jones's " 'official' myth about Ferenczi and Rank serves to eliminate the only two productive and imaginative disciples among the original group who had remained after Adler's and Jung's defections."[7]

If Jones, Fromm says, was unfairly critical about some of Freud's followers, he was far too uncritical about Freud himself. With rare, and brief, exceptions, Fromm's own criticisms of Freud previously had been directed toward ideas and not the person. But in this new climate of "hero worship" surrounding the publication of Jones's biography, he took a different tack. In his *Saturday Review* article he asserted that he had no intention of accusing Jones of "conscious insincerity"—but what about "unconscious strivings"? The time seemed ripe for Fromm to do what Jones had done only sparingly: to turn psychoanalytic techniques upon the founder of the method itself. In *Sigmund Freud's Mission*, published in 1959, Fromm attempts precisely that.

Freud, he says, had enormous belief in the power of reason, and remarkable self-discipline. But he was essentially unable to be warm and loving with others on anything resembling an equal basis. The absence of these qualities, says Fromm, helped account for Freud's de-emphasis of feeling and affect, and for his corresponding overemphasis on a rationalistic approach to man. Accounts of these personal qualities, and their presumed origins and implications, dominate *Sigmund Freud's Mission*. An understanding of them, Fromm suggests, is useful to correct the one-sided uncritical portrait of Freud offered by Jones, and it also may lead to a more clear comprehension of Freud's major theories on human frailty, sexuality, and the discontents of civilization. In other words, Fromm seeks to place Freudianism in a personal context and, more briefly, in a socioeconomic context. The book cannot supplant Jones's, nor is it really intended to (it is only a little over a hundred pages long); but it provides, as Bruno Bettelheim and others have commented, a useful and provocative additional perspective.

Fromm begins, like any good Freudian, with a discussion of home and mother. In Freud's first great work, *The Interpretation of Dreams*, Freud supplied only two dreams about his mother. Judging from those and from Freud's autobiographical comments, Fromm sees no reason to doubt Jones's conclusion that Freud had deep love for, and great attachment to, his mother. But Fromm feels Jones was quite unanalytic about this relationship since he ignored the concurrent dependency pattern. This dependency, as well as insecurity, says Fromm, is revealed again and again in Freud's relations with his wife, friends, and followers. One key source for Fromm is the intimate letters that Freud wrote to his longtime friend, Wilhelm Fliess. These letters, as well as others subsequently published, have led some writers, including Philip Rieff, to question many of Jones's interpretations. In one letter to Fliess, for example, Freud expressed a desperate fear of impoverishment; in several others he spoke sadly of his "emptiness." Neither Freud's mother, nor his wife, for all the support they afforded him, could ever allay these gnawing fears—the kinds of fears that Freud himself had described as typical of the insatiable, oral-dependent character.

Fromm argues that the insecurity cloaked an inability to love very deeply. Freud, he insists, had to maintain complete control in his love relationships. With his wife Martha, he was a jealous lover, going so far as to insist she withdraw affection from her own family. Autobiographical writings reveal that he always seemed too busy to spend time with her. Freud's rationalizations to cover both his domination over and his neglect of Martha were so obviously in the male egocentric pattern, says Fromm, that he finds it incredible that Freud and Jones remained so blind to them.

From Freud's letters and comments about his diminished or exhausted "libido," as well as his theories about the limited satisfactions of sex, Fromm concludes that inhibited sexuality in Freud's own life contributed to his broad, and biased, generalizations. In one of his articles, Freud made a rather typical—for him—comment, that after "three, four or five years marriage ceases to furnish the satisfaction of the sexual needs that it promised." And his attitudes about female sexuality betray an astonishing ignorance about women. Fromm quotes from a letter to Marie Bonaparte in which Freud remarks: "The great question that has never been answered, and which I have not been able to answer, despite my thirty years of research into the feminine soul, is what does a woman want?"

Repeating a comment he made in earlier writings but now placing it in context, Fromm says that the great spokesman for sexual liberation was essentially a puritan. Independently, Philip Rieff was arriving at the same conclusion: for Freud, he says, "pleasure is defined, after the manner of Schopenhauer, as a negative phenomenon." Rieff's view is that Freud "comes to the tacit understanding that sex really is nasty, an ignoble slavery to nature." Rieff is quite correct in saying that Freud's views on sex cannot simply be ascribed to his sharing the Victorian ethos, and he suggests more complex social and cultural determinants.[8] Fromm's evidence also moves in this direction in a later section of his book.

From Freud's dependency attitudes toward his mother and his wife, Fromm then considers, in an extension of his *Saturday Review* article about Ferenczi and Rank, Freud's relationships with colleagues. The pattern was always the same, says Fromm: an intense friendship, then a sudden break—often accompanied by outright hatred. It happened with Breuer and with Adler.

With Fliess and Jung, Freud suffered curious symptoms: am-
nesia, when Fliess complained that Freud had appropriated
one of his ideas (bisexuality); fainting spells, when Jung's dis-
agreements became too intense.

The compulsive need to be loved and to dominate fit together
for Fromm into a pattern of authoritarianism. What was Freud's
relation to his father?—ambivalent, marked by resentments
that Papa Freud was not a greater, more significant person. Here
then, says Fromm, are the classic elements of the Oedipus
complex: excessive attachment to the mother, resentment and
jealousy of the father as usurper. No wonder that Freud, from
his own childhood experiences and from the reinforcing experiences of the Vienna middle-class neurotics who were his early
patients, projected an Oedipal construct into the whole human
situation. Jones, says Fromm, never seems to discern these
things; but other analysts, such as Ferenczi and Hanns Sachs,
sometimes did.

Fromm then develops the thesis made explicit by the book's
title, *Sigmund Freud's Mission*. The boy who had admired
Hannibal and political acquaintances who became powerful and
committed leaders of German Socialism, later transferred his
identification to Moses, the great messianic leader of the Jewish
people. As self-styled "messiah," then, Freud helped create the
psychoanalytic "movement." For details of this process, Fromm
can rely directly on Jones. To insure tight control, especially
after Jung's defection, Freud founded a secret international
committee with six of his closest and most trusted associates.
"It would make living and dying easier for me," Freud wrote to
Jones, "if I knew of such an association existing to watch over
my creation. First of all: This committee would have to be
strictly secret in its existence and in its actions...." When
the committee fully assembled a year later, each member received an antique Greek intaglio for mounting into a gold ring
—like the ring Freud himself had long worn. And in later
writings Freud employed political terminology to describe the
movement, referring to the "motherland" and "colonies" of
psychoanalysis and to the need to "fortify our dominion."

The final step, in Fromm's analysis, came when Freud's followers fully institutionalized the "movement" by adopting
Freud's precepts as unassailable dogma (Fromm's own first
article, back in 1927, supplied a nice example of the properly

humble tone). These followers organized a "ritual" around the couch, established the specific time duration of analytic sessions, asserted the analyst's imperturbable silence, and so on. And they submitted to "idolization of Freud's personality" to complete "the picture of the quasi-political character" of psychoanalysis. It is a devastating, albeit somewhat comic and caricatured picture that Fromm draws. But anyone acquainted with orthodox psychoanalytic procedures recognizes certain elements of truth; Fromm might have mentioned here, although he doesn't, that counterparts might be found in a wide variety of other social, religious, scientific, educational, and other "movements" in our corporate society. It is worth noting, too, that Fromm's analysis of dogma, ritual, and idolization, all in ostensibly depoliticized forms, may help supply another explanation why certain scholars, especially those of the so-called myth-and-symbol persuasion, have been so committed to Freudian orthodoxy.

There is one more dimension to Fromm's analysis: socioeconomic context. Some years earlier, David Riesman, in *Psychiatry,* had perceived the similarity between Freud's pleasure-pain conception and the "scarcity" theories of the classical economists.[9] Thinking along identical lines, Fromm suggests that a whole range of Freudian theories are not revolutionary at all; instead they are conservative reapplications of nineteenth-century capitalistic thinking (much as American Social Darwinists applied biological "laws" to social and political institutions). Freud's doctrine of "sublimation," for example, is seen as quite similar in structure to the middle-class myth about capital formation: "Just as wealth is the product of saving, culture is the product of instinctual frustration." Again, the competitiveness and aggressiveness that were imputed to "human nature" by nineteenth-century tooth-and-claw theorists are neatly transferred by Freud to his analysis of culture: "Civilized society," Freud said, "is perpetually menaced with disintegration through this primary hostility of men towards one another." Freud's libido theory, supposedly biological, has a curiously "economic" aspect. It is always a "fixed quantity" with absolute limits on expenditure.[10]

Fromm does not attempt in *Sigmund Freud's Mission* to present the more dynamically positive side of Freud, the aspects of his thought that in so many ways have had revolutionary

implications for human conduct and understanding. The book
is one-sided much of the time, and its brevity and repetitiveness
suggest that it was put together rather hastily. But, although a
more balanced picture would have made for a more impressive
book, Fromm had a more specific objective. Clearly, his intention
was to remove Freud from the pedestal on which his idolators
had raised him, so that he might be recognized as a human
being with very real weaknesses and limitations. An occasional
reviewer recognized this. M. F. Ashley Montagu commented
that Fromm's book was "admirable" and that it "helps the
reader to a more profound understanding of Freud and the
quasi-religious-political nature of orthodox psychoanalysis."

III *On War and Peace*

After *Escape from Freedom,* all of Fromm's books had been
published during the Cold War years—a period not yet past,
of recurrent international crises, domestic witch hunts, and the
ever-present threat of nuclear holocaust. This era surely tries
men's souls; and, as the revival of Freudian purism indicates,
it also tries the beliefs that man is essentially "good" and that a
"sane society" remains achievable. No wonder, some writers
suggested, that Fromm had moved increasingly toward religion
and mysticism, had begun to stress the "limits" of reason. To
grasp for the self-transformation of satori, said one critic, hints
that Fromm may have despaired of the possibilities of social
transformation. Fromm himself had argued in 1931 that when
the revolutionary spirit of first-century Jews was crushed by
Roman power, many had turned to "fantasy gratification," to the
other-worldly redemptive promise of John the Baptist.

But Fromm, whose paradoxes have puzzled many readers,
now presented another one to confound his critics. Soon after the
publication of *Sigmund Freud's Mission,* and even as the work
on Zen was appearing in print, Fromm forthrightly entered the
public discussion of foreign policy. The paradox is more apparent than real: Fromm's diversity of interests has never really
narrowed; he has always kept in close touch with contempo-
raneous events; and he has always been convinced that private
and public worlds are intimately related.

After forty years of considering himself a Socialist but never
committing himself to party affiliation, Fromm not only joined

the American Socialist party, taking an active leadership role
with Murray Kempton, Irving Howe, Upton Sinclair, and others,
but he even wrote a "Socialist Manifesto" intended for a party
platform. In articles and books over the next several years,
Fromm's emphasis turned sharply from a search for self-
transformation to a militant call for social action. He still
believed, he announced unequivocally, in the necessity of "ultimate concern," because the robotized, bureaucratized society was
still very much with us. But in 1960 the immediate threat was
thermonuclear war, and the passions of bellicosity were accel-
erating all the worst tendencies of the insane society. Russians
and Americans alike were locked in "frozen stereotypes," prison-
ers of nonfunctioning ideologies that militated against any
realistic interpretation of what the "other side" was like. In
calling for drastic rethinking of American beliefs, Fromm ante-
dated by some years the proposals of Senator J. W. Fulbright
that Americans reexamine "old myths" in the light of "new
realities."

Recognizing that complete unilateral disarmament was clearly
unacceptable at this time to most Americans, Fromm argued in
Daedalus magazine for what Charles Osgood has called "graduated unilateral action" toward disarmament. Osgood had
advocated a step-by-step policy, one widely publicized, which
would clearly indicate America's pacific intentions toward the
Soviet Union. Such a policy would minimize the threat America
posed to the Soviet and would, he hoped, induce reciprocal
action. Fromm admitted the plan was inherently risky. But were
the risks greater, especially in a "gradual" approach, than continuing the present suicidal course of the arms race?

America's present foreign policy, he argued, not only brings
the country to the abyss of total war; it is driving it ever deeper
into dehumanization: "The real threat to our existence is not
Communist ideology, it is not even the Communist military
power—it is the hollowness of our beliefs, the fact that freedom,
individuality, and faith have become empty formulas. . . . Instead of experiencing love of what we are *for*, we experience hate
of what we are against."[11]

The primary resistance to changing America's course, Fromm
says, springs from fear that the Soviet Union seeks to conquer
the world for Communism. But, he insists, the monolithic
view of Communism as a system of belief and practice that has

remained immutable through time and space is fallacious. Only the bare bones of Marxist-Leninist ideology remain intact: the Leninist vision of world "conquest" was abandoned in the early 1920's. The Soviet Union in 1960, he says, is a conservative, class-ridden regime: "The ruling class of the Soviet Union is no more revolutionary than the Renaissance popes were followers of the teachings of Christ." In fact, he argues, the security of the Russian ruling class is jeopardized by genuine revolutionary movements in other parts of the world; one day, Russia's position vis-à-vis a "potentially expansionist China" might be very like the current American attitude toward Russia.

Of course, he concedes, it is *possible* that Russian leaders are irrational and are plotting to destroy American civilization by force or subversion—just as it is *possible* that a paranoic is correct in believing that his wife, family, and friends are conspiring to murder him. But is it sane to stake everything on this possibility, when so much evidence could be marshaled against it? If, says Fromm, Americans are going to deal in a sane and realistic way with personal affairs or public problems, they ought to be concerned with *probabilities*.

A year later, in 1961, Fromm expanded the themes from this article into a full book, *May Man Prevail?* As the interrogatory title indicates, Fromm poses a challenge in this work: are men able, are men willing, to examine in depth their cherished beliefs about capitalism, Communism, and war? Fromm once more is fusing two "disciplines," this time along the line charted out by Harold Lasswell. Men's political beliefs, Fromm argues, verge on pathology. They are victims, he says, of "projective" thinking; "the enemy appears as the embodiment of all evil because all evil that I feel in myself is projected on to him." A cathartic function is served, but the pathological approach to political reality is a "dangerously explosive psychological mixture." As in *The Sane Society*, Dr. Fromm's patient is the public itself—and not only Americans, but all of the peoples caught up in the "common craziness" of the Cold War. People should pay attention, Stuart Chase said in a review, to Fromm's "excellent" linkage of politics and psychology. If they would, he thought, "our chance of escaping Doomsday would be markedly improved."

Fromm insists that there are no insuperable barriers to communication and coexistence between America and the Soviet

Union. Those who depict the nations of the "free world" as
angels, and Communist countries as devils (or vice-versa) have
no awareness of history and no operational sense of modern
socioeconomic realities. Despite apparently antithetical ideologies, both America and the Soviet Union are essentially conservative, materialistic, managerial societies. And both are far
more interested in achieving international stability than in
promoting world revolution. Khruschchev, he says unequivocally,
"neither needs nor wants war."[12]

But of course, Fromm notes sadly, most Americans would
disagree fervently and would label such comments "heresies,
nonsense, or subversion." They believe, as their ancestors did
about witches, that there is ultimate—perhaps supernatural—
villainy afoot. Modern man, smug in the hindsight of history
and comfortable with the fruits of progress, recognizes that
Medieval witch-hunters were pathological, that there really was
such a phenomenon as an "insanity of millions." But modern
man exempts himself; he is convinced that his impeccable rationality immunizes him from such extreme psychic distortion.

As Exhibit A for those who doubt that men can conceal mad-
ness beneath the veneer of rationality, Fromm offers Herman
Kahn's well-known study, *On Thermonuclear War*, with its
balance-sheet approach to genocide. Kahn assures his readers
that a pretty good percentage of people could survive an
atomic attack; perhaps "only" five million deaths would occur
if all precautions—fall-out shelters, tactical evacuation, and
so forth—were taken. It should be difficult for any sane man, even
without Fromm's detailed indictment, to read Kahn's book without revulsion. But Fromm does a thorough demolition job. He
points out the unreliability of Kahn's statistics; the naïve
optimism that relies so heavily on the efficacy of "precautions";
the apparent unawareness that weaponry becomes increasingly
more sophisticated and destructive; the psychological innocence
that fails to question the effects of mass destruction even on
those who manage to survive. Above all, Fromm stands "amazed"
at the moral cretinism of the entire "genocidal" position. But
Kahn is not unique. How many people, Fromm wonders, have
descended to similar moral bankruptcy? He cites the familiar
case of the "murderous bureaucrat," Adolf Eichmann, and a
newspaperman's sudden recognition that in this creature who
calmly signed the death warrants for countless innocent Jews,

"one suddenly hears speaking the faceless 'company man' of the oversized industrial organization, the alibi-ridden, buck-passing, double-talking, reading-by-ear personality who has been drained of native emotion and principle and filled with an unreal ideology."[13]

For Fromm, the greatest obstacle to coexistence in 1960 was the question of German unification. The West argues that Russia has nothing to fear from a reunified Germany because the Germans since World War II have become peace-loving, democratic people. Fromm is as skeptical as the Russians are, because the same power structure that propelled the Kaiser and Bismarck backed Hitler and the Nazi party, and the same industrial and military potential is alive today. In addition, says Fromm, German nationalism persists; and it is fanned continually by the German political leadership, which waves "reunification" at the German population. The whole reunification question, he believes, is a sacred cow, and artificial to begin with: the unification of Germany is a recent invention, less than one hundred years old. To accede to it is to play the German game once again, as England and France did in the 1930's with Hitler. There is only one road to German reunification, he says; and the Germans know it full well: war.

Failing to understand national differences led Americans, Fromm believes, to a disastrous attitude toward Castro's "authentic Cuban revolution." By stressing Castro's Communism and isolating Cuba, this country forced him into hostility toward it and into alliance with Russia. American predictions about his Communism were almost classically "self-fulfilling." America, says Fromm, must abandon clichés about East and West, accept the status quo, push for universal disarmament, and recognize the "neutralist" concept instead of the "you-are-with-us-or-against-us" mentality of the late John Foster Dulles. Fromm believes that America must grant the right of countries to create their own political structures—and give them the kind of economic and technical assistance that they need to do so. America cannot force its brand of "democratic capitalism" on under-developed countries who neither want it nor are capable of achieving it. But the time for such realizations is growing short, Fromm warns. He argues psychoanalytically that "unconscious defeatism . . . a lack of faith in the very values which we claim" lies deep-seated beneath present American thinking. "Unless we act soon ... circumstances, institutions, and weapons, which we created, will take over and decide our fate."

Fromm's proposals for a reorientation of American foreign policy were not dramatically original. But they were lucid; and, although one might quibble about particulars, they were eminently sane. Lucidity and sanity on these matters were rare qualities, even among the "experts," in 1960. In his role as minor prophet he seems to have done rather well in predicting the take-over by "circumstances, institutions, and weapons"; apologists for America's frustrating involvement in Vietnam have, by hindsight, blamed precisely such "intangibles."

IV *Karl Marx and "Humanistic" Socialism*

In one of several documents Fromm wrote at this time for the Socialist Party-Social Democratic Federation, he cited the goal of nineteenth-century Socialists: to free man from economic bondage, and to enable him to function in a humane and dignified relation with his fellow man. But these purposes had largely been perverted, said Fromm, by Socialists who had gravitated toward statist, regimented social structures and by Socialists who had accommodated themselves to the various new faces of advanced capitalism. It was time, he said, to return to first principles. In a "Socialist Manifesto," he offered his own list.[14]

The "supreme principle," he argues, is that man, his life, his purposes, his work, and his creation must take precedence over things, goods, capital, and "circumstances." Every man is responsible for all fellow men; therefore production, consumption, and political structure should all be directed by man's needs and man's purposes. Decentralization of activities, wherever possible, is imperative. Finally, economics should be "reduced to its proper role as the means to a humanly richer life." As "intermediate goals," Fromm urges not only participant control of enterprises but also central planning and nationalization of basic industries where socially useful. Incomes need not be equalized, but they ought to be leveled so that great disparities in "life experience" do not exist. National sovereignty and the armed forces should be abolished; racial and sexual equality (but not "sameness") should be established; and critical thinking should be encouraged through all of our cultural and educational media.

Darlington Hoopes, national chairman of the Socialist party, noted that Fromm's paper was greeted with enthusiasm by some and "a certain amount of dissent" by others. In the 1960 election, a tiny minority of the electorate voted Socialist. But change was necessary, Fromm believed; and he still had faith in the uses of history. At the conclusion of *May Man Prevail?* he remarked that "historical trends have to be understood and anticipated." Such a statement was, of course, very remote from the spirit of Sigmund Freud, whose approach to history was at best ambivalent and at worst, as Philip Rieff terms it, "disrespectful." Fromm's historiography has been in the line of Karl Marx, who argued that man was creator and created: man made circumstances and history, and circumstances and history made man.

Marx had always figured prominently in Fromm's thinking. As we have already seen, Marxian dialectics, Marxian class analysis, and Marxian socioeconomic reasoning had threaded their way through the fabric of Fromm's work for over thirty years. It was Marx's term "productive" that identified Fromm's single positive character type, and Marx's concept of "work" was embedded in that productive character. Marx's dynamic analysis of alienation was intrinsic to Fromm's own extended analysis of the sick, or insane, society.

But Fromm had quoted Freud far more frequently over the years; nearly every topic Fromm had discussed at length began with a résumé of Freud's contribution. Now Fromm's immersion in Socialist activity and his concentration on topical problems seem to have provided the impetus for him to organize systematically his ideas about Marx. In 1962 Fromm brought out two books. The first, *Marx's Concept of Man,* contained Fromm's long essay on Marx's ideals and ideas, published together with a large selection, newly translated by T. B. Bottomore, of Marx's not very well known *Economic and Philosophical Manuscripts* and other early documents and letters. The second book, *Beyond the Chains of Illusion,* placed Marxian and Freudian ideas side by side for purposes of comparison, contrast, and synthesis.

Marx's Concept of Man was very different in its intentions from *Sigmund Freud's Mission.* In his study of Freud, Fromm had tried to undermine slavish devotion to orthodoxy by dissecting the motivations and the underlying ideological structure that helped to shape Freud's theories; he sought to demolish the myth that Freud had been almost devoid of personal limitations and immune to cultural pressures. The case of Marx was different. Fromm felt that Marx's ideas had been grossly misrepresented; his intention was to "rectify" widespread distortions about them. In no way was Fromm attempting a biographical sketch of Marx himself.

Marx, says Fromm, has been caricatured into a narrow "positivistic-mechanistic" social scientist, whose theories allegedly lent themselves to the regimentation, uniformity, and depersonalization of man. How ironic that such an interpretation should come from American readers, Fromm remarks, because "the very same reasons which are said to be proof that Marx's ideas are incompatible with our religious and spiritual tradition and which are used to *defend* our present system *against* Marx, are at the same time employed by the same people to prove that capitalism corresponds to human nature and hence is far superior to an 'unrealistic' materialism."[15] Fromm's argument is similar to the one Thurman Arnold had used a generation earlier in *The Folklore of Capitalism* to defend the allegedly evil governmental action of the New Deal against the allegedly noble behavior of unrestricted private enterprise. Fromm, like Arnold, is suggesting that fossilized ideologies and popular belief have little connection with social realities and even less with "human nature."

The real Marx, says Fromm, was neither a philosophical idealist like Hegel, nor a "vulgar materialist"; rather, Marx produced a new philosophical synthesis concerned with the *whole* man. Marx offered for the first time a "detailed analysis of institutions as being rooted in the mode of production and the productive forces underlying it." To this analysis, says Fromm, Marx coupled an all-encompassing vision of the relation between man and nature, with productiveness ("labor") as the mediating factor.

Fromm stresses two Marxian concepts that have been central to his own theories of man: productiveness and alienation. He argues that by productiveness, Marx means the "process of genuine activity," in which work is a means to an end (the product) and also an end in itself as a "meaningful expression of human energy." Capitalism is fundamentally wrong, therefore, not only because it leads to an unjust distribution of wealth but because it perverts labor into meaningless activity and thus transforms man into a "crippled monstrosity." Under capitalism, labor has become alienated: "work has ceased to be a part of the worker's nature." Things and circumstances, which man himself has created, become rulers over him. All man's other achievements, including ideas and art, have become similarly perverted. Fromm agrees with the common charge that Marx failed to predict the astonishing growth of the "middle class," but insists that this unexpected historical development simply lends *more* sweep to Marx's basically correct diagnosis: Marx failed to "foresee the extent to which alienation was to become the fate of the vast majority of people, especially of the ever-increasing segment of the population which manipulate symbols and men, rather than machines."

For Marx then, Socialism was not the goal but the means, not "the fulfillment of life, but the condition for such fulfillment." In later years, Fromm admits, Marx changed some ideas and concepts (the newly translated manuscripts date from the 1840's). Marx and Engels were well aware, he says, of how idealistic and religious terms could conceal economic and social realities. They abandoned terms like "species" and "human essence," and Marx certainly became far more pessimistic as he grew older. But, Fromm insists, the basic affirmation of man remained intact; there was lifelong "continuity" in Marx's fundamental beliefs.

That the early works of Marx conveyed these humanistic, even "idealistic" sentiments, no sophisticated reader can deny. But some Marxist scholars expressed strong reservations about Fromm's book. One lengthy review, for example, appearing in *Studies on the Left*, questioned Fromm on three major points: that he misgauged his audience; that he underestimated the importance and depth of Marx's development; and that, by stressing "idealistic" values, Fromm placed Marx in such uncongenial company as Paul Tillich, religious mystics, and Zen Buddhists. A. James Gregor, author of the review, felt that Fromm was attacking a straw man. Who could believe that Marx was a crude materialist, he asked, except "incredibly uninformed, impossibly naïve, or unredeemably biased" people? And such people, he argued, could hardly be influenced by such a book as Fromm had written.

Gregor seems off-base here. David Riesman, for instance,

writing in *The American Scholar,* and James L. Adams, professor of ethics at Harvard, wrote of being struck by the "scope of the humanist side of Marx" and by Fromm's "arrestingly fresh interpretation." Not everyone interested in Marx is a scholar in depth; and the early manuscripts, which had not been published in English until the 1930's, had never been widely circulated. As to education of the "uninformed," Fromm had raised the question years before of just how many laymen, including educated laymen, really were "informed" about Marx. Fromm's "educational" effort was another demonstration of his refusal to accept the belief that most people are "unredeemably biased."

A potentially more valid reservation raised by Gregor was textual—how real was the "continuity" in Marx's thinking? Fromm admits that Marx changed his mind on some matters after 1844 and that he wrote later of "settling accounts with an "erstwhile philosophical conscience." Gregor argues that the mature Marx greatly modified his perspective, but really answers his own question by raising another one: "How and how much of this youthful sentiment infused itself in the later Marx is a problem which can only be carefully and laboriously explicated."[16]

Fromm, by stressing Marx's humane value system, hoped to add his own voice in advocacy of "humanistic socialism." A considerable body of literature on this subject has been produced in the last decade, especially in Europe. In 1965, in fact, Fromm was to edit a volume of such writing, under the title *Socialist Humanism.* That it covered a wide range of perspectives was clearly demonstrated by the inclusion of an article by Fromm's old adversary, Herbert Marcuse. Marcuse, who like Fromm has long been intrigued by the intellectual brilliance of both Marx and Freud, has attempted his own synthesis. So have many other scholars, despite the facts that Freud considered Socialism hopelessly idealistic and that Marx certainly would have branded psychoanalysis as bourgeois individualism.

The conflicts between the ideas of Marx and Freud are obvious, but so, too, for the careful reader, are important points of convergence. Having incorporated for years so many ideas from both men, "correcting" the limitations of each with insights from the other, and having written small books on both, it was entirely appropriate for Fromm to write a direct comparative

study. In *Beyond the Chains of Illusion,* Fromm places the ideas
of Marx and Freud side by side on topic after topic, very much
as he had done with the ideas and methods of Zen Buddhism
and psychoanalysis.

Fromm's Marx is clearly the superior figure: Freud cannot
even be compared in "stature . . . and historical significance."
Marx's thought had far "greater depth and scope." In fact, Fromm
always has been somewhat ambivalent in his estimate of Freud.
In early writings, he hewed strictly to orthodox Freudianism. In
the 1940's and 1950's, as one historian of psychoanalysis writes, it
was easy to see where Fromm disagreed with Freud; the hard
task was finding where he *agreed* with him. Another writer
accused Fromm of having "a running feud" with Freud for
twenty years. In his most recent writings, Fromm says he feels
he has "moved closer to Freud." At one point in *Beyond the
Chains of Illusion,* he calls Freud a "liberal reformer" as con-
trasted with Marx, the "radical revolutionist." But on another
page he calls Freud's system "radical" too, and "revolutionary"
in the sense that it "opened up a new era of thought."[17]

But Fromm does find that Freud and Marx share many
"common premises." Both shared a lifelong skepticism about
"clichés, ideas, rationalizations, ideologies." Both were exemplars
of the humanistic tradition, believing that each man represents
all of humanity, with the concomitant motto: "Nothing human
is alien to me." Both offered dynamic and dialectic approaches
to reality—one by psychoanalysis, the other by socioeconomic
analysis. Both felt that the prime forces governing man operated
"behind his back," that observable phenomena were not only
inadequate but often completely misleading.

Perhaps their fundamental source of disagreement lay in their
notions of basic reality. For Freud, says Fromm, it was the
individual's libidinous organization; for Marx, it was socioeconomic structure. Thus, Freudian man was a model constructed
in the image of a machine; and Marxian man was a given potential, a product of history who could transform it and himself.
Freudian man evolved individually through libido stages, and
collectively into civilization through "sublimation." Marxian man
evolved historically and dialectically; his individual evolution
took place inside that historical process.

For Freud, "human nature" was essentially psychological,
predicated on sexual release and repression or, in Freud's later

theories, conflict between life and death instincts. "Human nature" for Marx was built around productivity, the practice of life rather than inner, relatively fixed psychological components. Their analyses of man's sickness and health revolved around the same constructs. Freud charted out Oedipal conflicts as the origins of neurosis. Marx had no systematic psychopathology but identified alienation from self and others as "*the* sickness of man." Freud pictured unrepressed primitive man as possessing precivilized health; adult, "genital" man was a shadowy conception, who actually seemed, says Fromm, "the concept of a well-functioning member of the middle class at the beginning of the twentieth century, who is sexually and economically potent." Marx took a Spinozan view, posing "activity" versus "passivity" as the criterion for defining mental health. Health is rooted in the act of self-creation, independence, productivity.

On close inspection, says Fromm, these apparently antithetical views are often mirror images of each other, almost metaphorically so: "Freud's independent man has emancipated himself from the dependence on mother; Marx's independent man has emancipated himself from the dependence on nature." Yet Fromm consistently implies that Freud's is the narrower view, that he, more than Marx, was circumscribed by the ideologies of his own age and by the limitations of his vision of man. Freud's dynamics had potentially universal implications, but they were highly individualized and mechanistically oriented. Marx's dynamics swept through evolutionary historical forces, socioeconomic processes, modes of activity, and the individual "practice of life."

Pushing beyond both Marx and Freud, Fromm summarizes his own views on existential and historical dichotomies, and how "social character" dynamically bridges the gap between culture and private belief. He is newly emphatic about the prime importance of the "socially conditioned filter" through which only certain kinds of experience can enter awareness. Through an array of linguistic and cultural mechanisms, social forces determine consciousness—and largely imprison men inside distorted, or false, understandings. Men intellectualize at the expense of feeling; they confuse words with the reality behind them. To these corruptions of truth, Fromm concludes, have been added the terrible effects of mechanization and militarization. But man's heritage is still available, he insists; and Marx and Freud remain guideposts for the searching, humanistic mind: "If we should all perish in the nuclear holocaust, it will not be because man was not capable of becoming human, or that he was inherently evil; it would be because the consensus of stupidity has prevented him from seeing reality and acting upon the truth."

CHAPTER 7

Toward a Synthesis of Idea and Action

I *Critics and Doubts*

B Y THE early 1960's Fromm had written about a dozen books, many of which had sold widely; but one looked in vain for anything resembling critical consensus about his place and value in modern thought. Three lengthy critiques of Fromm's work were written between 1961 and 1963, each founded on a radically different set of assumptions.

Martin Birnbach's *Neo-Freudian Social Philosophy* (1961), to begin with, is moderate and pragmatic in tone. Birnbach discusses six figures in some detail, but Fromm comes in for the fullest analysis. Birnbach's book is impressive for its scope and care, and also because he manages consistently to remain dispassionate. Whatever Birnbach's personal predilections, he tries to understand Fromm and the others in their own terms, rather than to evaluate them against some arbitrary standard. His hesitancy about pronouncing final, sweeping judgments is a refreshing antidote to the dogmatic assertions that have marked so much criticism in these highly problematical areas.

Birnbach's over-all judgment of Fromm parallels his general estimate of the "Neo-Freudians." It is mixed—or perhaps the precise term is "balanced." He finds Fromm socially programmatic in ways and depth that are not characteristic of other "Neo-Freudians," but he believes Fromm's programs suffer from a lack of economic and political realism. Similarly, while Birnbach believes that Fromm may "exaggerate the value of love," this error ("if any") is "one of emphasis, not of direction." He finds Fromm too utopian, too "original," and too attached to natural-law philosophy to propose realistic solutions. But, at the same time, Fromm's assault on capitalist social institutions is seen as "cogent," an indictment convincing enough to justify serious attempts at reconstruction. Birnbach believes that the methodological contribution of Fromm and the others (not so much the interdisciplinary approach per se as the insistence that people be the "ultimate subject matter of inquiry in the social sciences") will have more impact on social thinking than their substantive ideas—but this belief is "tentative."[1] Birnbach, then, is cautious; his yeas and nays often are succeeded by a "but, on the other hand—." And the framework by which he judges ideas is somewhat circumscribed: the book gives practically no indication that Burckhardt, Weber, Rank, or Bachofen lay significantly in the background, or, for that matter, that biblical prophetic ideals and the mystical tradition have been major influences on Fromm's conceptions of life, love, and the sane society.

By contrast with Birnbach, John H. Schaar's *Escape from Authority: The Perspectives of Erich Fromm* (1961) suffers from little humility, false or otherwise. Schaar's special expertise is in political and ethical philosophy, and he finds Fromm's positions woefully inferior to his own. For Schaar, man is a slight creature; and while it would be nice to see his condition improved, one should not expect overmuch: "Men will be ruled. The majority of men lack the power to form their own conceptions of the real and the ideal." Hence, leaders must formulate ideals and must impose "uniform and authoritative rules." Fromm, of course, begins with an almost diametrically opposed assumption about men; his ideal of democracy consists of lifting man's own capacity to determine the good, and to organize the conditions under which he lives. Schaar interprets this intent to mean that Fromm would dispense with *all* authority; hence he comments that "the greatest failure of Fromm's thought is that he cannot see ... that when authority is lacking fashion reigns." For Schaar, such a situation means anarchy, chaos.

Schaar may have had one eye on Berkeley, where he has taught, and where campus demonstrations (about which he has written caustically) helped start a chain reaction in many other schools. At any rate, he has taken some aspects of Fromm's thought, truncated them from the main body of thought, and equated them with the anarchist element that sometimes can be detected in New Left philosophy. By this distortion, Schaar arrives at the palpable absurdity that Fromm's "productive man" may well be a "beatnik." That Fromm's "productive man" is, by definition, committed to meaningful *work* seems to have escaped Schaar's notice. The reasons are not hard to find. Schaar likes order; he is devoted to precise, fixed categories of thought. It is for him a "fact" that, while life and death represent a purely empirical question, living well or poorly suggests a purely ethical question. It is a "fact" that mental health is a purely moral concept. For Schaar, there is no breaching the boundary between ethics and esthetics: these are "different subjects, each with its own canons." He finds that Freud and Fromm have an "absolute" difference on the question of civilization and its discontents. Lines are always clear: Fromm *must* choose either this or that, *must* go "forward or backward."

For Schaar, also, the history of ideas is filled with absolutely closed issues: "Marx gave away the show . . . ," or "Hume gave away the secret . . . ," or "Hegel is right . . . ," or "Esthetic criticism must start from the premise that . . ." With such a categorical approach to ideas, Schaar cannot really understand Fromm at all. Unlike Birnbach, Schaar never seems to understand the important role that "emotion" plays in Fromm's thought; he largely ignores the dialectical matrix in Fromm's outlook, and most of the psychological and psychoanalytic underpinning of Fromm's work. While Schaar continually argues that Fromm is unscientific, he accepts as uncritically as do some literary critics the essential soundness of Freudian libido-instinct theory. Unsurprisingly, the orthodox *Psychoanalytic Quarterly* was very pleased with his book, and convinced that "the psychoanalyst" would agree with Schaar's conclusions.

Schaar does raise a number of important questions about Frommian propositions which seem dubious and about Frommian contradictions which can be troublesome, especially in regard to the nettlesome concept of "self" and the weaknesses of the model "sane society." But even here, while Schaar acknowledges no previous critics of Fromm, these arguments had been made in substance years earlier by critics like Arnold Green, Henry Kariel, and Paul Tillich. Sometimes, even Schaar's phrasing sounds reminiscent of earlier writers.[2] Perhaps the chief difficulty raised by the book, the factor that tends to undermine Schaar's more acute assessments, is one of temperament (Edgar Friedenberg has called the book "unbearably snide"). Rather than questioning Fromm's ideas, Schaar usually dismisses them. He finds Fromm's theory of love "wrong," Fromm's critical theory

"a failure," Fromm's utopianism "blind," Fromm's theory of
work "inadequate," Fromm's notion of abundance "incompre-
hensible." Fromm, he charges, "is a moralist with no conception
of the moral life." Schaar seems unable to recognize that there
may be important truths in such statements as these by Edgar
Friedenberg: "I think Fromm makes an unanswerable case for
the existence in all men of very strong tendencies toward free
and spontaneous growth." Or, Fromm is "justifiably skeptical
of both the power and the inclination of secular authority to
further the ends of love and human justice."[3]

Harry K. Wells, in *The Failure of Psychoanalysis* (1963), disagrees with Fromm as firmly as Schaar does, but from very
different premises. Indeed, as a Pavlovian and strict materialist,
Wells takes immediate and permanent exception to the idea
that there is even such a thing as the "unconscious." But, unlike
Schaar, he recognizes the role it plays in Fromm's thinking, he
shares awareness of dialectical processes, and in some important
ways he shares Fromm's humanitarian (although not Fromm's
"humanistic") ethos. The structure of Wells's book follows what
he might call the "internal history" of psychoanalysis. He begins
with Freudian tenets and the dissemination of Freudianism;
glances briefly at early apostates; moves on to "reformed"
psychoanalysis (concentrating on Horney and Fromm); and
then, in discussing "reconstruction" of psychoanalysis, specifically
concentrates on Fromm's theories of love and alienation. From
Wells's historical perspective, psychoanalytic theory had reached
a hopeless impasse by the mid-1940's, and Fromm was the
principal spokesman attempting, futilely, to redirect it toward
fusion with existential philosophy and the New Theology.

Wells's argument is an articulate statement of the behaviorist
position, or at least the Pavlovian branch of it; and it clarifies
some important opposition to psychoanalytic theory. He insists
that only historical conditioning makes scientific sense. The
"heart of Freudianism," as he sees it, is that Freud, at a time
when cerebral physiology was floundering, postulated an "unconscious" to account for and accommodate the phenomena of
blurred or lapsed memory. Unproved and unprovable, this
theory, says Wells, has been undermined rapidly by the building
of a "science of higher nervous activity." The "labyrinthine"
and "mythical" construction of innate racial memory and of the
libido-instinct theory is no longer tenable in the light of what

is now known scientifically: "The mind *is* the functioning of the brain, nothing else." The conditioned reflex, the "cell" of mental activity, is the functional base on which "the entire complexity of animal and human activity is constructed."[4] From these premises, Wells finds to be futile not only classical psychoanalysis but all attempts to "reform" or "reconstruct" it. Reformers Horney and Fromm sought to inject a social dimension, to label the society itself "sick," and thus to transfer the causative burden. But, says Wells, this attempt ends in a cul-de-sac, with no possibility of any rational and productive human beings being produced. All that is left of social-individual connections is "the pseudo-medical one of traumatic shock producing a neurotic condition."

Fromm's final leap, says Wells, was to reconstruct Freudianism on "humanistic lines," to resuscitate "essential" qualities—inherent needs and abilities to love, rooted in the unconscious. As an alternative to the despair of his age, Fromm, like other "isolated" and forlorn humanists in theology and philosophy, returned to faith. But regression to the notion of an "indwelling soul," whether in biological or divine terms, merely demonstrated the emptiness of the presuppositions of psychoanalytic theory in toto. Wells, incidentally, turns out to be more optimistic than Fromm. Where most of Fromm's severe critics suggest that bleaker images of man are more "realistic," Wells finds renewed hope in the dialectics of history. He would wish not for a purer Freud but for a purer Marx—of whom he is almost totally uncritical. As for the counter-critique of behaviorism by Fromm, this will be discussed in conjunction with *The Crisis of Psychoanalysis*, published in 1970.

But one point of convergence between Fromm's theories and behaviorism might be observed, as it occurred in *The Heart of Man*, which Fromm wrote in 1964, a year after Wells's study. Fromm is tussling, in one section of this book, with the hoary philosophical dilemma of choice and determinism. He concurs with William James that, while this conundrum may never be resolved, one still may profit by "deepening our sense" of it. One cannot, he argues, talk sensibly about "freedom of choice" between "good" and "evil" in *general*. One can only talk meaningfully about the individual man and about his "concrete and specific actions toward what is good [or] what is evil, provided good and evil are properly defined." Further-

more, one is not dealing with an "absolute" question—the problem is one of the "conflict of inclinations and their respective
intensities." These in turn hinge on the individual's character
as it has developed until a given moment. So "freedom of choice,"
as Fromm defines it operationally here, is in one sense an
orientation rooted in character structure. In another sense, it
is a capacity to make a choice between opposite, morally loaded
alternatives.

The decisive factor in the choice, says Fromm, lies in awareness of what constitutes good and evil, of what is the appropriate means to the end, of the necessity for action. Only up to a
certain point in the wish to stop smoking, in the course of a
potential seduction, in a game of chess, or in war, are there
"real possibilities" for moral choice. Since decision-making oppor-
tunities arise continually, Fromm points out, each individual
choice can strengthen the character along positive or negative
lines. Interestingly enough, Fromm's careful explication of the
habit-forming dynamics of man's decision-making process is
startlingly analogous—in different terms—to behavioristic
theories of conditioning. The psychologies of Harry Wells and
Fromm, beneath their layers of theory, may have more common
ground than either antagonist can recognize or admit.

In 1964, when *The Heart of Man* was written, Fromm did
feel that he was moving closer in mood to Freud. "As one whose
views have been often misrepresented as underestimating the
potential of evil within man," he wrote wryly, "I want to
emphasize that such sentimental optimism is not the mood of
my thought." In 1961 in *May Man Prevail?* he had deplored
the increasingly pervasive "genocidal" mentality of the cold
war era. That same year, in an address before the Seventh
Inter-American Congress on Psychology, he began formulating
a constellation of negative psychological traits. His topic was
the "revolutionary character," the truly free man, a dynamic
version of the "productive character." As opposed to the "revolutionary character," who "loves and respects life," Fromm mentioned briefly another type of personality, one attracted by
"death, destruction, and decay." Such a character, he said, "can
be called necrophilous, to use [Spanish philosopher] Unamuno's
expression in his famous answer ... to a Franco general, whose
favorite motto was 'Long Live death.'"[5] In 1963, in reviewing
a posthumous work by Carl Jung, Fromm speaks of being "im-

pressed by Jung's deep affinity for death, destruction, the past, the dark, ice, stones and everything that is not alive. Blood and corpses, skulls and murder are the repetitive theme of his dreams." Fromm notes that "this was not all of Jung," but the syndrome here represented a "necrophilous complex."[6]

These brief references first achieved a theoretical formulation in a short study Fromm wrote that year, under the working title "On the Psychological Causes of War." He argued that there is a "secondary" tendency in man, one he called "necrophilia," which works in destructive opposition to the primary tendency toward life-sustaining and life-expanding attributes, "biophilia." Actually a collection of syndromes based on traits that were rooted in lesser or greater degree in everyone's potential character, necrophilia, Fromm said, was more widespread and intense in the nuclear age. When Paul Tillich and Hans J. Morgenthau criticized this study, charging, respectively, that Fromm had overemphasized psychology and underestimated the crucial role of "power structures," Fromm denied that he had committed the "fallacy of psychologism"; he was trying, he said, to understand "the human factor . . . among the conditions which make war possible." Human destructiveness, he agreed with his critics, certainly was not *the* cause; and he changed the essay's title to *War Within Man: A Psychological Enquiry into the Roots of Destructiveness* for release in bound form.

Fromm's expansion of these ideas appeared in 1964, as the major section of *The Heart of Man*. Fromm still rejects the Freud-Menninger concept of the "death-instinct," a concept that anthropologist Geoffrey Gorer says "in part confirmed de Sade's pessimistic diagnosis of 'man's loathsome heart.'" Nevertheless, considering the mass brutality of the twentieth century, Fromm feels one should not underestimate man's "propensity of evil." Some "deep indifference to life," he suggests, lies in the "deeper layers of the personality." But if there is no destructive instinct, what then are the fundamental dynamics behind violence? Fromm theorizes a "syndrome of decay," comprising three orientations: "the love of death," "malignant narcissism," and a "symbiotic incestuous fixation." Pure character types are rare, he points out (Jung's impulses toward creativity *and* destruction represented a "peculiar balance"); but, still not yielding to angst, Fromm continues to insist that the fundamental tendency of all living organisms is to live and to grow.

Love of death, the "necrophilous" orientation, is thus a secondary potentiality, a "malignant" phenomenon that arises when the specific conditions for human growth and freedom are absent or inadequate. A dialectic (on both economic and psychological planes) is played out between health and psychopathology, in the conditions of exploitation-equality, justice-injustice, concern-indifference, concrete living-abstractification and mechanization. Fromm agrees with Freud that narcissistic tendencies are universal, but he insists that there are both benign and pathological forms. An optimal amount, he says, serves a biologically useful purpose—survival—and, kept at a level compatible with social cooperation, narcissism can lead to interest in one's own work, to a "self-checking dynamic," to creativity. But narcissism can also reach pathological peaks, generating megalomania and xenophobia. Pathological "group narcissism," as exemplified by Nazi attitudes toward Jews, or by the attitudes of poor whites toward Negroes, manifests an ideology of superiority that ultimately is destructive for everyone.

The final destructive orientation is "incestuous symbiosis." In Freud's interpretation of the Oedipal triangle, the boy's sexual desires for his mother are repressed because of the father's strength; the boy in turn identifies with the father. Fromm reverses the Freudian scheme, emphasizing the "natural" pregenital needs for protection and unconditional love. Two polar tendencies are present from the moment of birth, says Fromm: to "emerge to the light" and risk independence, or to regress toward the securities of comfort, protection, and dependence. Some fearful and lonely people regress to cults: the Great Mother, the Virgin, or irrational patriotism. Like narcissism, regression has benign and malignant forms. Franklin Roosevelt, suggests Fromm, was "moderately mother-fixed" as well as "moderately narcissistic." The deepest level of the mother-fixation is "incestuous symbiosis," where a host-parasite or even a *folie à deux* relationship can ensue. When the various malignant forms of the three orientations are blended, we have the "syndrome of decay," and the archetype is Adolf Hitler.

The opposite, healthy syndrome is the "syndrome of growth," demonstrated by biophilia rather than necrophilia, love rather than narcissism, independence as against incestuous symbiosis. If one pieces together Fromm's varying interpretations and categories, the "biophilous" character seems like the "productive" character with, perhaps, "revolutionary" traits added. The "necrophilous" character has no precise antecedent, but it obviously is shaped out of Fromm's "nonproductive" traits and his "thing"-oriented mode of "assimilation." His discussions of negative human characteristics are provocative and systematic, and probably, to a degree at least, redress the imbalance of human character that "realist" critics called for. But there is a clinical dryness in *The Heart of Man* that is very atypical of Fromm's writing. In a way, these pages form a grim counterpoint to *The Art of Loving,* but the difference in tone is startling. One suspects that Fromm, unlike Jung, is not at all fascinated by morbidity, and his writing lights up as soon as he leaves the subject.

II *From Tradition to Innovation*

If a new demonstration were needed that Fromm continued to trust the old humanistic values, it was provided by his next book, *You Shall Be as Gods,* in 1966. In general, the book's tenor is that of religious modernism, following the methods of symbolic interpretation and evolutionary theism that were first systematized by the Higher Critics of the Bible in the late nineteenth century. In this respect, as a reform rabbi commented, there was not much "new or revolutionary" in Fromm's study. But when before, the rabbi asked, had a psychoanalyst ever undertaken such a careful and sympathetic exegesis?

"Sympathetic" really is an understatement, for Fromm avers that the Bible is "an extraordinary book, expressing many norms and principles that have maintained their validity throughout thousands of years. It ... has proclaimed a vision for men that is still valid and awaiting realization." So, for Fromm, traditional wisdom still finds practical application in the modern world. The Old Testament, he says, is, and remains, a "revolutionary" book. The biblical prophet as revolutionary is, of course, an old conception as Fromm himself points out. Among examples of modern literature, a work which make this point most explicitly, as well as paralleling such other Fromm themes as equalitarianism, an anti-war spirit, the ideal of "rebirth," and excitement in living

for life itself, is Clifford Odets's 1935 play, *Awake and Sing!*
(The title itself is a quotation from Fromm's favorite prophetic
figure, Isaiah.)

Fromm, the atheist, finds it imperative that the reader of *You
Shall Be as Gods* understand his approach to "God." The concept
of God, he says, "was a historically conditioned expression of an
inner experience," a concept given to the "x-experience" (a
Fromm neologism for theistic or nontheistic "religious" feeling)
in many places around the world between 1500 B.C. and 500 B.C.
It was the belief in a *ONE* who represented "supreme value and
supreme goal for man." Fromm then recapitulates his arguments from *The Art of Loving* about the evolution of "God"
from anthropomorphic being down to (or up to) the *"nameless*
God" and the "negative theology" of Moses Maimonides; with
that step, there is nothing one can say or think about *God* at all.

Man, imbued with "x-experience" (or "reverence for life,"
in Albert Schweitzer's term), can embody the humane attributes
that, in an earlier age, he affixed to a literal God. He can become
like God, but he can never *become* God. Human history recorded
in the Bible follows, for Fromm, an evolutionary course parallel
with that of the concept of God. It begins with the separation
from home (Paradise), and it proceeds to the universalism
implicit in such texts as the Book of Ruth. Never, says Fromm,
does the God of the Old Testament impel the move toward
man's freedom by "changing his heart," by intervening in history. Man must make his own history. Typically, Fromm offers
two examples: one from the Book of Exodus and one from today's
front pages. In Exodus, the miracles performed by Moses and
Aaron could not change men's hearts; indeed, the Jews regressed to idolatry again and again. Today, says Fromm, the
"free world" and the "Communist world" have so far restrained
themselves. But they have not yet recognized that the threat
of force will not guarantee peace and that force will not solve
the real problems. Their joint suicidal course "only hardens
man's heart more and more, until he arrives at the point where
he ceases to care; at this point he will act as did Pharaoh, and
perish as did the Egyptians."

As for the role of the Prophets, it is, says Fromm, to reveal
truth, but not truth as an exclusively spiritual idea. The prophets
operate inside history, for the "God of history"; hence they must
be political men too; they *have* to be dissenters and revolution-

aries. And they point toward the next step in history, the messianic time. Then man, left homeless after Paradise, will recover his home: the world itself. He will be "fully born." He will end his struggle against his fellow men and nature, and establish a new and profound harmony. The Prophetic message is neither determinism (beyond man's conscious control) nor pure will (totally within man's control); rather, says Fromm, it is a realistic set of predictions based on close knowledge of how human hearts actually are or are not hardening. Fromm, in short, is applying the theory he had outlined in *The Heart of Man*, a fusion of determinism and free will to which he had given the unfortunately ungainly name of "alternativism."

Near the end of *You Shall Be as Gods*, Fromm writes about the Sabbath, the anticipation of the messianic time, the symbolic liberation from the chains of time, and the moment of reunion between man and man, and between man and nature. Thus does Fromm in 1966 return to the Fromm of 1927, and to the very first topic he had ever written about, "The Sabbath," and calls again for affirmation.

A sociopolitical context for reaffirmation appeared a few years later in the revolt against President Johnson's Indochina policies and the vigorous grass-roots campaigns conducted for Senators Robert Kennedy and Eugene McCarthy. The signs of resurgent hope for change were "clearly visible," said Fromm. He now wrote what was in effect a sequel to *The Sane Society*, a book titled *The Revolution of Hope: Toward a Humanized Technology*.

Fromm's updated critique of contemporary America was not essentially different from what he had written fifteen years earlier. We were facing, he said, the specter of total mechanization, in which "we will nothing, nor do we not-will anything." He found himself in company with an old humanistic ally, Lewis Mumford, who in *The Myth of the Machine* defined the "megamachine" as the completely systematized, homogenized, and pervasive social system, and with the French critic Jacques Ellul, whose *Technological Society* was a devastating, although largely pessimistic, analysis of the same phenomenon. And Fromm renewed his assault on his old "emotion-free" bête noire, Herman Kahn. In *May Man Prevail?* Fromm had attacked Kahn's balance-sheet approach to thermonuclear war. Now he attacks Kahn's *The Year 2000* as "alienated megamachine" thinking. Readers, he said, mistook "thousands of little data . . . for erudition or profundity. They do not notice the basic superficiality in his reasoning and the lack of the human dimension in his description of the future."

According to Fromm, megamachine thinking, as symptomatized by Kahn but widespread across American life, centers around a narrow and crippling concept of "efficiency" which leaves out man himself and what he needs for healthy human functioning. Fromm cites such "pathogenic" symptoms as a blind belief in the efficacy of computerized planning, impersonal calculation of human needs, and the increasing popularity of social and biological scientists who overstress man's animalistic propensities. In the last-named category he singles out Konrad Lorenz's *On Aggression* and Desmond Morris's *The Naked Ape*. Fromm is not unaware of the controversies concerning man's evolutionary heritage, and the way they focus on the conflict between the neocortex and the more primitive "old" brain. He admits he can only "guess" at the truth, although he cites one scientific authority, Ludwig von Bertalanffy. Fromm's feeling is that "particular relations between the large neocortex and the old brain are the basis for . . . specifically human feelings."

Regardless of the biological truth about this question, Fromm argues that man the system, with his particularly human qualities, must be at the center of any social planning and organization. He draws on the structure he had outlined in *Man for Himself* and *The Art of Loving* to delineate his own conception of what man is and what man needs.

Grounds for hope always remain, Fromm says, as long as there are realistic possibilities. Certainly "hope" can be founded on illusion; he finds the term as paradoxical and complex as "faith" or "freedom." Basically, he believes hope to be an "inner readiness, that of intense but not-yet-spent activeness," In one of his more poetic passages, his naturalistic and mystical conceptions are neatly entwined: "We cannot say that the tree 'hopes' in the same way in which a man hopes, since hope in man is connected with feelings and awareness that the tree may [*sic*] not have. And yet it would not be wrong to say that the tree hopes for the sunlight and expresses this hope by twisting its trunk toward the sun. Is it different with the child that is born?"[7] There was dissatisfaction in the land in 1968, and some of it was channeled into what Fromm saw as important social and political protest. Realistic grounds for hope were present.

How can hope be put to work to achieve a more humane way of life? Fromm cites four "givens" which he insists must be taken into consideration: the necessity for much centralized enterprise, much centralized planning, cybernation, and a realistic appraisal of man himself. We must have a greater knowledge of what man is, we must have humanistic management of public concerns, we must have active engagement of people in all the processes which affect them, and we must recognize that there are no absolutes in questions of freedom versus control or centralization versus localism; experience and mutual intelligence can help us to find optimal measures.

More specifically, Fromm eschews violent revolution, sabotage, and words tossed into the wind; he rests his own hopes on face-to-face dialogue and democratic organization. He proposes as a basic mechanism for change an elaborate system of associations which vary in size, function, and scope. In some ways it is a political counterpart of the economic cooperative he discussed in *The Sane Society,* but more comprehensive. Boimondau, the economic cooperative, had been offered as a paradigm; now Fromm suggests a fully national network. He urges the formation of a national council of about fifty enlightened and responsible citizens to raise issues, gather information, and presumably lobby for legislation; a system of local councils to generate support and ideas; clubs to discuss issues and stimulate public activities; and "groups" to pioneer new styles of life and new philosophies. All of these associations would somehow interweave although they would not be formally bound together.

The "group" concept, he carefully notes, would represent a deeper, more committed way of life than might be found in an "encounter group" or a transient hippie commune. Yet a reader might be struck by the parallel between Fromm's thinking and patterns of interaction that already had taken root by 1968. Similarly, John Gardner's "Common Cause" resembles Fromm's idea of a national council that acts as a broadly based American conscience, gadfly, and citizens' lobby. The activities of Ralph Nader and of various voluntary and municipal consumer-action groups are at least steps in the direction of a "consumer revolution" which Fromm has urged, not only in *The Revolution of Hope,* but as far back as *The Sane Society.* In 1960 Fromm had contributed to Socialist party efforts: in 1968, although he clearly still was committed to Socialism as an ideal, he sympathized strongly with the insurgency of Senator Eugene McCarthy inside the Democratic party. One of Fromm's associates, Michael Maccoby, took the biophile-necrophile hypothesis from *The Heart of Man* and applied it in a study of popular attitudes toward Presidential candidates. Using a random sample of 160 Californians, Maccoby reported that 77 percent of the McCarthy supporters exhibited "love of life" characteristics, compared with 46 percent of the Rockefeller partisans and a slender 27 percent of the Nixonites. The election results did not offer an encouraging diagnosis about the heart of the American people.[8]

III   *Character in Time and Place*

Among the principal charges leveled against Fromm's writing over the years were: (1) that his work lacked any strong empirical base; was too heavily built on unsubstantiated theory and speculation; (2) that his work was too cross-disciplinary; for while scholars may welcome insights from fields other than their own, depth in a single discipline is essential for a clear focus; (3) that he was too individualistic, refusing to pay serious attention to scholars who worked in allied or even identical fields. The first and last of these charges seem to have had some basis during most of Fromm's career. The second may never have had any validity; rather, it seems to reflect a bias that has less and less currency as old, artificial barriers between "fields of study" have broken down.

But a long-promised study by Fromm, finally published in 1968, offered a solid rebuttal to all three criticisms. In *Social Character in a Mexican Village,* Fromm demonstrated his ability to work collaboratively with a wide range of scholars, to incorporate substantial research including sophisticated statistical method, and to justify his cross-disciplinary approach if the intention was to investigate life styles in depth.

The study's basic intention was to test Fromm's "social character" theory, the comprehensive man-in-society formulation first presented in *Escape From Freedom,* and further developed through the elaboration of character types in *Man for Himself* and *The Heart of Man.* Secondary purposes were to apply psychoanalytic method to the testing of groups rather than individuals, and to seek clues for the planning of social change.

This ambitious project required a massive team effort, although the theoretical structure, with relatively minor additions, remained Fromm's. His principal collaborator, and the coauthor of the book, was Michael Maccoby, who shared Fromm's interests and perspectives, was trained by him in psychoanalysis, and subsequently performed other research in the area of social character. Fromm's original plan to investigate a Mexican village was conceived in 1957; Maccoby joined him in 1960; over the years, other assistance was afforded by psychiatrists, psychologists, anthropologists, statisticians, physicians, and a number of other specialists. The data collected and analyzed ranged through history, economics, social activities, health practices, personal attitudes, and, for depth studies, interpretive assessments of Rorschach tests, Thematic Apperception Tests, Anderson story tests, and dreams. For comprehensiveness, the book was like nothing else Fromm had ever published; it more nearly compares (even, in a curious way, in some of its final conclusions) with Robert and Helen Lynd's classic investigations of the 1920's and 1930's, *Middletown* and *Middletown in Transition.*

Fromm selected a village, unnamed (like "Middletown," which turned out to be Muncie, Indiana) but representative of many agricultural communities in southern Mexico. It was an *ejido,* a village founded in 1923 at the close of the Mexican Revolution, where the villagers were given small plots of land. From Fromm's perspective, it would be edifying to discover how this new economic structure, coupled with a general trend toward industrialization, affected peasant character; this is no small question in a world which even today is over 50 percent peasantry.   o

The *ejido* peasants were individualistic, conservative, and suspicious, like peasants in most places. Their small land plots made them relatively independent people, "dependent only on nature and the market." Fromm and his team found that the peasants also were dignified, concerned about their sense of self and about being good people. Their central conflict was "between cynicism and hopelessness on the one hand and faith, often a childlike faith, on the other." Industralization had generated new pressures, not only for better techniques to work the land more efficiently, but also a necessity for cooperative effort.

Most of the peasants were young because life was hard and health was poor; many were illiterate; and only a few had accumulated any money or possessions. As the *ejido* was a small community (792 in 1960), there was much communal discussion and decision-making, although a comparatively small number of more prosperous residents assumed a strong leadership role. Relatively clear class distinctions might be made, although all ranked far below an American median standard of living. The town's history was one of immigration of former residents and numerous migrants from elsewhere who came to the new town that had replaced the old authoritarian hacienda structure. Few ex-peons were prepared, in skills or attitudes, to cope with postrevolutionary society.

Aside from all the data gathered in more traditional ways, the key to the study was the application of psychoanalytic testing; through projective tests and interpretive questionnaires, measures of "social character" were determined. The questionnaires, which were refinements of the type Fromm and his associates had used in Germany in 1931, provided findings which correlated very well with results from the Rorschach and Thematic Apperception tests. Then the massive data, incorporating sixty-three variables, most of which were character traits (Narcissistic, Exploitative, etc.) were subjected to factor analysis.

From the tables and charts, which are accompanied by painstaking analysis that reveals the familiar Frommian blend of economic, anthropological, and psychiatric ingredients, three primary character orientations are identified. The single most frequent is the nonproductive-receptive and its sources are seen to lie in socioeconomic structure and family relationships. Both the Spanish hacienda system and the Aztec society which preceded it were hierarchal, breeding dependence in peons as similar societies did for slaves and serfs elsewhere. The Aztec society was essentially patriarchal but Mexican society since the conquest has been basically matriarchal: the home is dominated by emotional ties to the mother, and Mexican Roman Catholicism embodies the same principle: "It is no exaggeration," say Fromm and Maccoby, "to say that for the Mexican peasant, the Virgin of Guadalupe (and many other Virgins of local significance) is at the center of religious belief." Lacking a paternal principle, the male villagers tend to dependency, repressed violence, and alcoholism. Alcoholism is a problem of such extent that it receives a full chapter in the book.

The second most common character orientation is productive-hoarding, a type more nearly resembling the individualistic, stingy peasants of southern Europe. For Fromm and Maccoby, the explanation for this sizable minority in Mexico lies in economics: the productive-hoarding character seems to reflect the "peasant mode of production, which sometimes proves to be stronger than the general feudal influence, but *only* when the peasant possesses his own plot of land."

Ranking third in frequency, and comprising about 10 percent of the villagers studied, is the dominantly exploitative character. These are prototypes of modern entrepreneurs, who have used to advantage the possibilities of the new capitalism.

All in all, Fromm and Maccoby conclude that the Mexican Revolution was not revolutionary enough to effect drastic changes in life style for most of the peasants, nor to have altered the majority of character orientations. When the Lynds returned to Middletown after a decade which saw the arrival of the Great Depression, they detected numerous changes in the way people lived but relatively few substantial changes in basic thinking. One suspects that Fromm and Maccoby's kind of depth analysis, had it been applied to Middletown, would have underscored the Lynd conclusions, and for parallel reasons: the ideals and myths of opportunity and free enterprise in middle America were grounded too deeply and pervasively to permit a drastic alteration in character.[9]

More than material change and education are required for significant character change. To Fromm and Maccoby it was both "important" and "startling" that neither education nor literacy was correlated with material success. The nature of work had not changed enough to make advanced skills in reading and writing significant. Nor did new cultural stimulation achieve much response from the unproductive-receptive villager. These additives, as Fromm had argued years earlier, were not enough for transformation.

What might be done? "Culture," education, more active entrepreneurs all bring little or mixed results to raising the general level of the population to more productive attitudes and lives. Based on experiences and experiments in the villages, the brightest ray of hope lies in the creation of cooperative political, economic, and social activities in which a sense of individual worth and achievement simultaneously is maintained, and even strengthened. The village has been the site of agricultural cooperatives, as well as of a home for orphans organized on humanitarian and participatory lines. In the course of the Fromm-Maccoby study, a village boys club was formed, experimenting with modes of fostering cooperative activity, critical thought, and honest dialogue. The results achieved by all of these ventures offered encouragement that there were systems which might make a difference.

Fromm and Maccoby felt that the study confirmed the usefulness and validity of social character theory, and of the kind of methodology they employed. Finding and implementing methods for change represent a much more complex set of questions. Social character, with its accumulated methods, ideologies, and values, is built up over long periods of time: Fromm and Maccoby estimate that it took 300 years for a basic change in the European social character. On the other hand, they believe that a consumer character (an orientation totally absent from the Mexican villagers studied) was developed in the American middle class in a single generation. To digress to the Middletown parallel, one might infer that a social character analysis, or perhaps even one along the lines of the Lynds' sociological framework, might have yielded more dramatic results if the two studies had been conducted in Indiana just before World War I and after World War II; the intervening years witnessed the advent of the consumer society.

And those years also were the period of massive penetration of new advertising techniques, high-pressure persuasion on a national level, and burgeoning mass media. Fromm was hardly unaware of the power of propaganda in history, as shown by his studies of church doctrine, of Nazi persuasive appeals, and of the creation of the American "marketing character." But now he took special cognizance of the impact of television: "Never before had it been possible to reach and penetrate people of all ages so effectively as by the electronic media. . . ." He maintained the familiar humanistic skepticism about what might be accomplished, because the media were privately owned, represented the ethos of an "alienated society," and were dedicated to profit rather than social purpose. Further, because the media encouraged passivity and mindlessness, it appeared that they could more readily change character for the worse than for the better.[10]

A few years later, Fromm examined connections between consumer culture and the development of matriarchal tendencies in the United States. He had argued in a number of articles and books over the decades that affirmation of matriarchal principles (universality, unity, peace) was urgently needed in Western culture. But in 1971 he finds the trend regressive rather than progressive: in the "consumer culture" vision, he says, "technique assumes the characteristics of the Great Mother, a technical instead of a natural one, who nurses her children and pacifies them with a never-ceasing lullaby" (in the form of radio and television).[11]

IV *Convergence and Independence*

According to the introductory article in a recent textbook, *Readings in Psychology Today,* Fromm is "the outstanding advocate of a humanistic approach in psychoanalysis." At this point it is worth examining the ways in which Fromm's ideas coincide with—and diverge from—those of his contemporaries in behavioral studies. To begin with, Fromm has always considered his work "scientific," although empiricists like Harry Wells and skeptical "realists" like John Schaar deny that Fromm's theories are adequately grounded in scientific procedures. In the kind of formulation that drives Schaar and Wells crazy, Fromm once referred to his own efforts as "the applied science of the art of living." In 1944 in "Individual and Social Origins of Neurosis," he said that science had to be understood as a history of errors, that is, of "rational visions" which contained the "seed of truth." This "seed" was temporarily veiled by the limitations of available knowledge at any given time.

A decade later, even as Patrick Mullahy was writing that Fromm had deserted empirical techniques for philosophy and moralism, Fromm turned up as a contributor to a volume of essays, *What is Science?* In the company of such renowned experts as Bertrand Russell, Julian Huxley, Jacob Bronowski, and Clyde Kluckhohn, he was selected to explain the scientific rationale for psychoanalysis. Fromm's basic argument was that the inferential nature of psychoanalysis paralleled the recent approaches of the physical sciences:

In essence, this new principle was that not sensory experience nor common sense nor tradition is a guarantee of the truth; that to grasp reality—outside of man and within him—we must know the nature and direction of forces which are not directly visible, but which can be inferred from the visible phenomena they produce. . . . Freud taught man to be objective and to be humble; to be skeptical toward his conscious thoughts; to probe for the truth hidden in his unconscious, rather than to be satisfied with what he consciously believes to be true.[12]

Fromm spoke of the psychoanalyst's patient accumulation of data, his framing of hypotheses which might be rejected, altered, or confirmed, and so on. There is, of course, some substance in this methodological argument; and many observers would agree that scientific approaches can be utilized in this process, both in the formulation of general theories and in the therapeutic reconstruction of a life situation.

Nevertheless, many scientifically minded persons argue that the psychoanalytic method fails to live up to some traditionally basic criteria of "science." Logician Ernest Nagel has put the case succinctly. An empirical science, he says, must be able to "deduce determinate consequences" from its theoretical assumptions. And "at least *some* theoretical notions must be *tied down* to *fairly definite and unambiguously specified* observable materials, through generally accepted rules of procedure." Nagel's comments, incidentally, came in a symposium on psychoanalysis, philosophy, and science staged in 1959. The gaps between the participants' attitudes were sometimes profound; and, as several speakers noted, the whole enterprise came close to disintegration.[13]

Similar problems have sometimes occurred in the question of collaboration between psychoanalysis and the social sciences. Here, the record is far more mixed because points of convergence have been discerned frequently by scholars from the various fields: social psychology itself represents an important merger of "disciplines," and the whole thrust of "Neo-Freudianism" has been to effect a fusion. But stubborn resistance also has been common. Psychoanalyst Karl Menninger has argued that each specialist should stick to his own specialty, and the sociologist Arnold Green has taken essentially the same position. Fromm's arguments against psychoanalytic orthodoxy are clear. by this point; as for social scientists, he has said that too many of them have slavishly and mistakenly imitated the methods of natural science. Arguing along lines resembling those of sociologist C. Wright Mills in *The Sociological Imagination,* Fromm charges that many social scientists have self-limited their research to problems that lend themselves to easy empiricism. They have refused, he says, to investigate the things that matter most: the crucial problems of "happiness, ethical motivation and destructiveness" in the contexts of character structure and social structure.

But there are other difficulties, some of which were highlighted by a conference in 1949 on "culture and personality," in which Fromm, Kardiner, Sullivan, and a group of distinguished sociologists and anthropologists participated. Substantial agreement was evident that interdisciplinary approaches were valuable; psychoanalysts, anthropologists, and social psychologists all seemed familiar with one another's concepts and methods, and many had collaborated on interdisciplinary studies. But the emphases of Fromm, Sullivan, and Kardiner diverged in important ways; and, as some observers of the conference noted sadly, the social scientists were in no position to choose among them.[14]

Behavioristic psychology, whether that of Ivan Pavlov or of his American counterpart John Watson, has consistently been hostile toward psychoanalysis; Harry Wells's *The Failure of Psychoanalysis,* already discussed, is a typical perspective. Fromm has taken a quite tolerant view of behaviorism, saying that many of its studies "are sound and ... enrich the science of psychology." He objects when behaviorists "make claims which they cannot substantiate." Psychoanalysts argue that Freud's methods were as scrupulous, detailed, and "realistic" as those of the behaviorist, and that the psychoanalytic method is capable of pursuing elusive "truths" into far deeper areas of human experience.

Psychiatrist J. A. C. Brown remarks pertinently that terminology itself can prove the worst barrier between theorists: "Even behaviorism in its use of the conditioned reflex demonstrates that the subject of the experiment is responding, not to the immediate stimulus as such but automatically—that is in one sense of the word, unconsciously—to its past associations."[15] In this context, two references to Fromm seem appropriate. One is a reminder of his own strong emphasis on the importance of the "filter of language," which powerfully determines how one

thinks and communicates. Another is Fromm's suggestion that
Freudian concepts might be considered metaphorically, and this
could apply to the concept of the "unconscious" itself. The unconscious can be thought of, says Fromm, not as a region, but
as a way of describing a continuously connected process, part
of the whole realm of mental activity.

If practitioners of psychoanalysis and behavioristic psychology
often tend to believe their fields are mutually exclusive, a different kind of convergence has been suggested. Harry Wells writes
that Fromm may be the "most articulate and influential voice" of
the humanistic currents of thought that seek a new direction
out of a "wilderness of crass materialism and conformity in
spurious values." Two anthologies from the 1960's pointed up
the "influential" quality and the "new direction" to which Wells
refers: *Man Alone: Alienation in Modern Society* (1962), and
Psychoanalysis and Contemporary American Culture (1964). In
both books, selections from Fromm are the lead-off essays; in
both, references to Fromm by other authors are extremely frequent; in both, the "suggested bibliographies" contain more
recommendations for books by Fromm than for those of any
other author. (Fromm is more modest, incidentally, in an
anthology which he edited with Ramón Xirau in 1968, *The
Nature of Man*; his selection from his own writings is brief,
and his bibliography includes the sharpest criticism ever made
of his work, John Schaar's *Escape from Authority*.)

Man Alone has a vast sweep, from Marx to Dostoevsky to
a broad spectrum of modern selections from psychiatry, philosophy, and sociology—all revolving around the theme of alienation in its meanings, pervasiveness, and implications. *Psychoanalysis and Contemporary American Culture* has much the
same focus: its reiterated concepts are alienation, anxiety, and
loneliness. Repeatedly in these essays, one reads statements
that strikingly resemble Fromm's. Carl Rogers writes that "to
a degree probably unknown before, modern man experiences
his loneliness, his cut-off-ness, his isolation both from his own
deeper being, and from others." Rollo May writes on the incursions of phenomenology and existential psychoanalysis, and
speaking for those who more or less share these positions, says
that "our chief concern in therapy is with the potentiality of
the organism. . . . the nature of man itself must be understood
as a basis for our science and art of psychotherapy." The analyst,

says May, must get to the root question, which is the patient's being able to experience fully that "I am I; I am this being with all the potentialities and possibilities that constitute this being, this I."[16]

Perhaps the strongest affirmation of the ideal of convergence comes in Abraham Maslow's *Toward a Psychology of Being.* Maslow asserts that "Freudianism" and "scientific psychology" are meaningless terms, mere "loyalty-positions." He calls for enlarging "the jurisdiction of science so as to include within its realm the problems and the data of personal and experiential psychology." To find out what man is and can be, one must bridge the gap between the worlds of science and the humanities. Maslow is optimistic about what he feels is an informal "coalescence," an increasingly important "Third Force," which has emerged as a wedge between orthodox Freudianism and experimental-behavioristic psychologies. His roster of this group includes, among others, Adlerians, Rankians, Jungians, Neo-Freudians, Talmudic psychoanalysts, Gestaltists, Rogerians, existential psychoanalysts, general semanticists, and such mavericks as Herbert Marcuse and Norman O. Brown.[17] Maslow's allusions to Fromm are all laudatory, and when he cites "basic assumptions" held by the "new point of view," they appear almost identical with Fromm's.

Equally striking as convergence is the way some novels of the 1960's centered on themes that have absorbed Fromm for many years—suggesting that people at least a full generation younger than Fromm have been struck by similarly responsive chords. Most relevant for novelistic themes have been the first section of *The Sane Society,* with its massive indictment of corporate institutions and values, and *The Art of Loving,* with its impassioned call for personal feeling and concern, and for deep human relationships. The "insane society" in its most blatant commercial aspects is scathingly satirized beneath the ebullient wit of Joseph Heller's *Catch-22.* The "insane society" in its most brutalizing psychological implications is condemned in Ken Kesey's *One Flew Over the Cuckoo's Nest,* and Kesey's metaphorical setting is appropriate: a psychiatric institution where the keepers (who enforce "adjustment" in the name of "democracy") are far more mad than the inmates. And the "insane society" as a mechanistic, militaristic, dehumanizing monolith is portrayed in surrealistic, philosophical terms in Thomas Pynchon's *V.*

Heller's alternative is a recognition of the right of decent survival; Kesey's, a militant quest for freedom; Pynchon's, the
capacity to care, to be "alive" rather than "inanimate."

Despite real parallels and talk of "convergence," it is not
quite accurate to say that Fromm's belief system fits together
comfortably with any of the various writers mentioned. Few of
the psychoanalytic theorists Maslow cites, for example, match
Fromm's strong emphasis on the weight of socioeconomic factors and of historical dialectics. Maslow speaks of the "total
collapse of all sources of values outside the individual," and he
says that "political democracy and economic prosperity don't
in themselves solve any of the basic value problems." Certainly,
in one sense, Fromm would agree; he concluded as much in
Social Character in a Mexican Village. But despite his own
emphasis on the "self," the "humanistic" conscience, and the failures of the affluent society, Fromm is too steeped in structural,
institutional analysis and in the live crises of politics and war to
abandon his concern for historical conditioning. At one time he
categorized "existentialist psychoanalysts" as "superficial"; in
the recent "Crisis of Psychoanalysis," he still does not seem
terribly impressed.

Fromm also continues to point up differences between his own
beliefs and those of his contemporaries. He is, for example, unhappy with Carl Rogers's term "client-centered therapy," because it seems to him that there isn't any other kind of therapy—
the alternative is a "narcissistic analyst." He finds himself in disagreement with Martin Buber because Buber found Adolf Eichmann "totally alien." No, says Fromm, every human being shares
every human characteristic: "I find Eichmann in myself because I
find everything in myself—even, if you please, a saint." While he
praises Erik Erikson's "significant contributions to the theory of
childhood," he believes that Erikson "has not gone as far as he
could have had he followed in a more radical way the consequences of some of his premises."

Fromm has problems, also, with many of the values and methods of the younger generation, even though they reject the "pre-
fabricated society" and preach the virtues of love. The young, he
says, have become "neomatriarchal" in their opposition to the
state and to automatic obedience to elders and man-made laws,
and in their vocal insistence on self-determination. But he feels
that too often these attitudes are "mere negation of patriarchalism

and a straight regression to an infantile pattern." In several articles in the last few years, Fromm has accused his old adversary Herbert Marcuse of being the spokesman for this "infantile regression," as well as for misunderstanding both Freud and the nature of freedom.[18]

Probably the principal point of difference between Fromm and many of today's youth is that in spite of his contemporaneity, Fromm stands solidly on the value of preserving the humanistic heritage. One suspects that neither the Talmudic nor the post-Renaissance Western traditions which are so fundmental to Fromm's thought—nor, for that matter, the Indian culture that lies back of Ravi Shankar—can mean much to the ahistorical "teeny-bopper" or the student militant who takes a leap into postliteracy without first having been nourished on those older, humane values. Fromm himself has made this distinction clear. He recently argued that "there must be no force to prevent people from the satisfaction of their desires, including drug addicts, or any kind of sexual activity, provided it does not do harm to other people." But, he cautioned, protests are not enough; youth must establish a "frame of reference" on which to build a hierarchy of substantial, tenable values. There are ways, in short, in which Fromm seems relatively conservative. Playing devil's advocate, a magazine interviewer asked him, "Isn't the element of the marriage relationship that insists on fidelity—isn't that an example of hypocrisy?" and "Would you urge youngsters to have sexual activities before marriage?" Fromm's answers to both questions were flatly negative. When married people change sexual partners, he said, the probable result is a sacrifice of intimacy: "people are not all that secure." As for "urging" youngsters toward premarital sex, Fromm's opinion was that "Nature urges them enough."[19]

Conservative and yet still radical in many ways, Fromm obviously remains a hard man to classify. A colleague observes that Fromm "preserves a great independence (his friends have been known at times to think him a trifle too independent!) which serves as a relief and a gadfly in these days of radar-directed society." But wherever he stands, Fromm continues to move, and to write. He is convinced that the central, all-subsuming, problem now is "the opposition between the love of life (biophilia) and the love of death (necrophilia)," and he has been preparing a book, *The Roots of Human Aggression*. As always, he is ambitious; this forthcoming book is seen as only one volume of a comprehensive study of "humanistic psychoanalysis" which will deal at length with theory, behavior, techniques of therapy, and related matters. Such a work, if it fulfills his expectations, might serve as an antidote to the organizational difficulties that have plagued Fromm's individual books through the years; he plans, additionally, to introduce more direct clinical material.

But it certainly is not too early to conclude that Fromm has been a most useful contributor to the humane values of his time—and at a historical moment when faith in man is desperately needed. Critics may quarrel, and sometimes justly, with the rigor of the "science" he has brought to bear on human behavior and institutions, and some humanists may legitimately have reservations about the validity of some of his humanistic "principles." But there should be no faulting his integrity, his dedication to scholarship, or his commitment to the democratic ideal. At times, his reach may indeed have exceeded his grasp, but, as Browning's Rabbi Ben Ezra remarked, that is what the human enterprise really is all about. In an age of violence and of despair about man's present and future condition, Fromm has declared that man can still redeem himself. At the age of seventy, he wrote: "Who can give up hope as long as there is life? Who can be silent as long as there are billions of human beings, living, breathing, laughing, crying and hoping?"[20]

Notes and References

Chapter One

1. Unless otherwise noted, biographical comments on Fromm's youth and family life are from letters written by Fromm to the author in 1966 and 1967.
2. *Beyond the Chains of Illusion: My Encounter with Marx and Freud* (New York, 1962), p. 5.
3. *Sigmund Freud's Mission: An Analysis of his Personality and Influence* (New York, 1959), p. 3. For a sampling of other interpretations of Freud's "Jewishness," see Philip Rieff, *Freud: The Mind of the Moralist* (Garden City, 1961), p. 325; Ernest Jones, *The Life and Work of Sigmund Freud* (New York, 1957), III, 237-40; Sam Keen, "Man & Myth: A Conversation with Joseph Campbell," *Psychology Today*, 5 (July, 1971), 37-39, 86; David Bakan, *Sigmund Freud and the Jewish Mystical Tradition* (Princeton, 1958).
4. Hans Gerth and C. Wright Mills, *Character and Social Structure: The Psychology of Social Institutions* (New York, 1953), pp. xiii-xiv, xix.

Chapter Two

1. "Der Sabbath" [The Sabbath], *Imago*, XIII (1927), 223 (my translation). Almost all of Fromm's other publications in German have since been translated into English.
2. "The Dogma of Christ," in *The Dogma of Christ and Other Essays on Religion, Psychology, and Culture* (New York, 1966), p. 5.
3. David Riesman, "Freud, Religion, and Science," *Individualism Reconsidered* (New York, 1964), pp. 401-6.
4. In a "dynamic concept of ideology," says the later Fromm, we must recognize that "man has longings and passions that are deeply rooted in his nature and in the very conditions of human existence." *May Man Prevail? An Inquiry into the Facts and Fictions of Foreign Policy* (Garden City, 1961), p. 121.
5. Herbert Marcuse, "The Social Implications of Freudian 'Revisionism,'" *Dissent*, II (Winter, 1955), 224.
6. Martin Birnbach, *Neo-Freudian Social Philosophy* (Stanford, 1961).
7. See for example Walter T. James, "Karen Horney and Erich Fromm in Relation to Alfred Adler," *Individual Psychology Bulletin*, VI (1947), 105-16.
8. John R. Seeley, "The Americanization of the Unconscious," in

161

Charles Rolo, ed., *Psychiatry in American Life* (New York, 1966), p. 149.

9. Quoted in Richard Heffner, "An Interview with Erich Fromm," *McCall's*, XCIII (October, 1965), 216. For Freud versus Horney on "female" psychology, compare Freud, *New Introductory Lectures on Psychoanalysis* (New York, 1933), pp. 161-75, and Horney, *New Ways in Psychoanalysis* (New York, 1939), Ch. VI. On reciprocal influence between Horney and Fromm, compare Gerald Sykes, *The Hidden Remnant* (New York, 1962), p. 95, and Clara Thompson, *Psychoanalysis: Evolution and Development* (New York, 1950), p. 196.

10. See for example the discussion of Buber's ideas on "friendship" and "egoism and altruism" in Paul E. Pfuetze, *Self, Society, Existence: Continuity in the Thought of Martin Buber and George Herbert Mead* (New York, 1961), pp. 178-79.

11. "The Method and Function of an Analytic Social Psychology" (1932), trans. in *The Crisis of Psychoanalysis* (New York, 1970), p. 116.

12. *Escape from Freedom* (New York, 1941), p. 277.

13. Martin Birnbach, *Neo-Freudian Social Philosophy*, p. 81. For a miniature "debate" between Fromm and Kardiner on the respective merits of "social character" and "basic personality," see their separate articles in S. Stansfeld Sargent and Marian W. Smith, eds., *Culture and Personality* (New York, 1949), pp. 3-4, 64.

14. The quotations and descriptions of methods and conclusions in this unpublished study are taken from Fromm's recapitulations in "The Revolutionary Character" in *The Dogma of Christ and Other Essays*, pp. 151-53; *Escape from Freedom*, p. 237; "On the Problems of German Characterology," *Transactions of the New York Academy of Science*, V, 2d ser. (1942-43), 83; and *Social Character in a Mexican Village: A Sociopsychoanalytic Study* (Englewood Cliffs, N. J., 1970), pp. 24-26.

15. Extensions of Fromm's psychoanalytic "history" appear elsewhere too, notably in *The Sane Society* (New York, 1955), where he examines the stages of capitalism.

16. *Escape from Freedom*, pp. 119, 132-35. There are obvious parallels in analysis and sometimes even in terminology with sociologically oriented studies that appeared a decade or so later: David Riesman et al., *The Lonely Crowd* (New Haven, 1950), and William H. Whyte, *The Organization Man* (New York, 1956) are the best known. Riesman argues that a new character type ("other-directed man") has emerged, and Whyte believes that a corporate-society "social ethic" has supplanted the Protestant Ethic. More recently, Charles A. Reich has suggested that all of these new character types, which he calls "Consciousness II," are being succeeded by still

another, "Consciousness III" (*The Greening of America,* Random House, 1970).

17. Both later pieces sought to clarify the methods of "social character" analysis. In a review of Richard M. Brickner's *Is Germany Incurable?* (*Saturday Review of Literature,* XXVI [May 29, 1943], 10), Fromm attacked analysis-by-analogy as he had done in *The Dogma of Christ.* In an exposition of his own approach, he listed three cardinal principles: the necessary linkage of attitudes and character traits; a dynamic concept of character; environmental conditioning ("German Characterology," pp. 79-80).

18. Karl Menninger, "Loneliness in the Modern World," *Nation,* CLIV (March 14, 1942), 317.

19. Ruth Benedict, review of *Escape from Freedom, Psychiatry,* V (1942), 111-12.

Chapter Three

1. John H. Schaar, *Escape from Authority: The Perspectives of Erich Fromm* (New York, 1961), pp. 63, 66.

2. *Man for Himself: An Inquiry into the Psychology of Ethics* (New York, 1947), p. 40.

3. *Man for Himself,* p. 45. The phrase "living productively," with all that implies for Fromm, is crucial. Political philosopher Henry Kariel ("The Normative Pattern of Erich Fromm's *Escape from Freedom," Journal of Politics,* XIX [1957], 640-54) attacks Fromm's political theory largely on the basis that Fromm asserts that the "drive for self-preservation" is the "one primary and final need." Birnbach correctly observes that "Kariel . . . sadly misconstrues Fromm" in this matter.

4. Walker Percy, "The Coming Crisis in Psychiatry," *America,* XCVI (January 12, 1957), 417-18.

5. Schaar, *Escape from Authority,* pp. 18-24.

6. See for example Abraham H. Maslow, *Toward a Psychology of Being* (Princeton, 1962), p. 147.

7. Harry K. Wells, *The Failure of Psychoanalysis—From Freud to Fromm* (New York, 1963), pp. 133-34, 171, 235-36.

8. J. A. Brown, *Freud and the Post-Freudians* (Baltimore, 1961), p. 15.

9. This discussion clearly presages key ideas of *The Lonely Crowd.* Fromm had known Riesman for some time, and he acknowledges Riesman's "many constructive suggestions" in the foreword to *Man for Himself.* Riesman acknowledges his own indebtedness to Fromm's writings in *Individualism Reconsidered,* pp. 40, 56, 345, 401-8.

10. Marcuse and Wells both make this point. So too does Arnold W. Green, in "Sociological Analysis of Horney and Fromm," *American Journal of Sociology,* LI (1946), 533-40.

11. "Discussion of Symposium," *Proceedings of the Fourth International Congress on Mental Health* (Mexico City, 1954), pp. 26, 28.

12. Patrick Mullahy, *Oedipus: Myth and Complex—A Review of Psychoanalytic Theory* (New York, 1948), pp. 332-33.

13. Review of *Is Germany Incurable?*, p. 10. On Freud's "reticent" and "therapeutic" moralism, see Philip Rieff, *Freud: The Mind of the Moralist*, esp. Ch. 9, "The Ethic of Honesty."

14. *Man for Himself*, pp. 167-71. The *Trial* has of course been worked over by myriad critics. A good summary of major interpretations, plus an esthetic theory that would enable Fromm's psychoanalytic exercise to fit alongside the others without necessarily contradicting any of them, is Joseph Waldmeir, "Anti-Semitism as an Issue of Kafka's Joseph K.," *Books Abroad* (Winter, 1961), 10-15.

Chapter Four

1. For good statements about the role of "faith" in psychology and psychotherapy see John R. Seeley, "The Future of Psychiatry," in Hendrik M. Ruitenbeek, ed., *Psychoanalysis and Contemporary American Culture* (New York, 1964), p. 425; and Walter Bromberg, *The Mind of Man: A History of Psychotherapy and Psychoanalysis* (New York, 1963), p. 12.

2. Viktor von Weizsaecker, "Reminiscences of Freud and Jung," in Benjamin Nelson, ed., *Freud and the 20th Century* (New York, 1967), p. 72.

3. Concise accounts of the ideas of Liebman and Sheen and particularly of Peale, together with a careful historical examination of their American antecedents, are in Donald Meyer, *The Positive Thinkers* (Garden City, 1965).

4. Sigmund Freud, "The Interpretation of Dreams," in A. A. Brill, ed., *The Basic Writings of Sigmund Freud* (New York, 1933), p. 308.

5. *The Forgotten Language: An Introduction to the Understanding of Dreams, Fairy Tales and Myths* (New York, 1951), p. 207.

6. See for example Ramón Sarro, "The Interpretation of the Oedipus Myth According to Freud and Heidigger," *Journal of Existential Psychiatry*, I (1961), 478-500, and Rollo May, "The Context of Psychotherapy," in Ruitenbeek, pp. 82-84. On a later occasion, Fromm was to reexamine Freud's famous case of "Little Hans," again challenging the Oedipal interpretation ("The Oedipus Complex: Comments on the Case of Little Hans," *The Crisis of Psychoanalysis*, pp. 69-78).

7. Fromm has tried to clarify the distinctions between him and Jung on this point. There is of course, he says, "only one ontological structure of the nature of man," so the idea of "universality" makes sense. But he feels that the fundamental questions posed by life are

few, and so too are the possible answers man might give. Hence, the number of symbols which are really "universal" must be small. (Quoted in Richard Evans, *Dialogue with Erich Fromm* [New York, 1966], pp. 39-40.) For Joseph Campbell's most recent statement, see Sam Keen, cited, pp. 35-39, 86-95.

8. "Remarks on the Problem of Free Association," *Psychiatric Research Reports*, II (1964), pp. 4-5.

9. Quoted in "Discussion of Symposium," p. 28. For accounts of the changing attitudes toward transference, the role of the couch in therapy, and related matters, see Clarence P. Oberndorf, *A History of Psychoanalysis in America* (New York, 1964).

Chapter Five

1. Eric and Mary Josephson, Introduction, *Man Alone: Alienation in Modern Society* (New York, 1962), p. 10.

2. *The Sane Society*, p. 69.

3. *The Sane Society*, p. 120.

4. *The Sane Society*, pp. 143, 193.

5. Patrick Mullahy, "Philosophical Anthropology vs. Empirical Science," *Psychiatry*, XVIII (1955), 399-409.

6. Paul Tillich, "Erich Fromm's 'The Sane Society,'" *Pastoral Psychology* (September, 1955), 14-15.

7. Martin Buber, *Paths in Utopia* (Boston, 1958), p. 149.

8. Fromm expressed agreement with most of Neill's "life-affirming" principles about growth, honesty, and independence. But he thought that Neill somewhat overemphasized "an artistic and emotional grasp of the world" at the expense of intellectual development, and also that his tendencies were too Freudian—with a consequent over-estimation of sex. (Foreword to A. S. Neill, *Summerhill* [New York, 1964], pp. ix-xvi.)

9. Is there really a basic human need for religion, in the Frommian sense? For a zoologist's affirmative response, see Desmond Morris, *The Naked Ape: A Zoologist's Study of the Human Animal* (London, 1967), p. 181.

10. "God is dead" was, of course, Nietzsche's phrase. Fromm's application bears little resemblance to the God-is-dead controversy involving Joseph Altizer and others a few years ago.

11. Quoted in *The Art of Loving* (New York, 1956), p. 25.

12. See Norman O. Brown, *Life Against Death: The Psycho-analytical Meaning of History* (New York, 1959), pp. 320-21; and Abraham Maslow, *Toward a Psychology of Being*, p. 164.

13. See Harry Wells, *The Failure of Psychoanalysis*, pp. 187-88.

14. Jakob J. Petuchowski, "Erich Fromm's Midrash on Love," *Commentary*, XXII (December, 1956), 549.

15. "Medicine and the Ethical Problem of Modern Man," in *The Dogma of Christ*, pp. 190, 193-94.
16. D. T. Suzuki, "Lectures on Zen Buddhism," in Fromm, ed., *Zen Buddhism and Psychoanalysis* (New York, 1960), p. 76.
17. "Psychoanalysis and Zen Buddhism," in *Zen Buddhism and Psychoanalysis*, pp. 96, 98, 108.

Chapter Six

1. Herbert Marcuse, "The Social Implications of Freudian 'Revisionism,'" p. 224. For substantially similar reasons, Norman O. Brown calls "Neo-Freudianism" a "catastrophe," while Igor Caruso says that Fromm can't understand that psychoanalysis must function under the rubric of the prevailing cultural neurosis.
2. "The Human Implications of Instinctivistic Radicalism," *Dissent*, II (Autumn, 1955), 348-49; Herbert Marcuse, "Reply to Erich Fromm," *Dissent*, III (Winter, 1956), 81. In recent years, Marcuse has increasingly politicized his arguments; his audience has widened considerably, to the point where he has been called a major philosopher of the "New Left" (see Theodore Roszak, *The Making of a Counter Culture* [Garden City, 1969], pp. 84-123). Fromm sees Marcuse's recent popularity as an unfortunate symptom ("Mother," *Psychology Today*, IV [March, 1971], 74-77).
3. See Philip Rieff, "The World of Wilhelm Reich," *Commentary*, XXXVIII (September, 1964), 55; and Leslie Fiedler, *Waiting for the End* (New York, 1964), pp. 93, 97, 99.
4. Stanley Edgar Hyman, "Psychoanalysis and the Climate of Tragedy," in Nelson, p. 182; Jacques Maritain, "Freudianism and Psychoanalysis: A Thomist View," in Nelson, p. 230.
5. Gerald Sykes, *The Hidden Remnant*, p. 88.
6. Christopher Lasch, *The New Radicalism in America, 1889-1963* (New York, 1965), p. 311.
7. *Sigmund Freud's Mission*, p. 147. Further documentation defending Ferenczi is furnished by Fromm in *The Crisis of Psychoanalysis*, pp. 8-12. Fromm's comment about the absence of "productive and imaginative disciples" is not entirely fair, since Ernest Jones and Karl Abraham were of that group.
8. Philip Rieff, *Freud: The Mind of the Moralist*, pp. 170, 171. Rieff also remarks (p. 203) that Freud "achieved a notable repression" about his relationship with his mother—"a repression which Ernest Jones accepts without question in his life of Freud."
9. David Riesman, "The Themes of Work and Play in the Structure of Freud's Thought," *Psychiatry*, XIII (1950), 1-16.
10. Several writers have also remarked on the way Freud absorbed a mechanistic biology into his theories, based on his own late-nineteenth-century medical education. Fromm cites some of these

writers in "Freud's Model of Man and Its Social Determinants," *The Crisis of Psychoanalysis*, pp. 31-33.

11. "The Case for Unilateral Disarmament," *Daedalus*, LXXXIX (1960), 1020.

12. The thesis that Soviet and American systems and attitudes are developing striking parallelisms is outlined explicitly in Urie Bronfenbrenner, "The Mirror-Image in Soviet-American Relations: A Social Psychologist's Report," *Journal of Social Issues*, XVII (1961), 45-46.

13. Quoted from the New York *Herald Tribune*, April 23, 1961, in *May Man Prevail?*, p. 198. This concept is developed more fully, historically, and philosophically, in Hannah Arendt, *Eichmann in Jerusalem: A Study in the Banality of Evil* (New York, 1964).

14. *Let Man Prevail: A Socialist Manifesto and Program* (New York [1960]). Among the other Socialist Party-Social Democratic Federation publications to which Fromm contributed at this time were *We Have a Vision . . . A Deep Faith* (arguments for joining the Socialist party), and *New America*, a Socialist magazine.

15. *Marx's Concept of Man (with a translation from Marx's Economic and Philosophical Manuscripts by T. B. Bottomore)* (New York, 1961), p. 4.

16. A. James Gregor, "Erich Fromm and the Young Karl Marx," *Studies on the Left*, III (1962), 92. One book-length study of the kind Gregor suggests does find contradictions of significance between the earlier and later views. The author concludes that Marx's "fundamental weakness" is a "failure to work out that distinction between freedom and servility in positive terms" (Eugene Kamenka, *The Ethical Foundations of Marxism* [New York, 1962]).

17. *Beyond the Chains of Illusion*, pp. 26, 135-36.

Chapter Seven

1. Martin Birnbach, *Neo-Freudian Social Philosophy*, pp. 231-32.

2. Schaar speaks satirically of the "green and gentle lands of Frommian perfection." Stanley Hyman earlier had referred, in "Psychoanalysis and the Climate of Tragedy," to Neo-Freudians "lying down in green pastures beside Norman Vincent Peale." Schaar praises "the mystery and grandeur of human beings," while Will Herberg, in "Freud, the Revisionists, and Social Reality," earlier had observed that Fromm can't see man "in both his 'grandeur' and his 'misery.' "

3. Edgar Friedenberg, "Neo-Freudianism and Erich Fromm," in Ruitenbeek, pp. 383, 379. Friedenberg, incidentally, concludes that Fromm is a "Manichean," an attitude which he says requires great optimism about man's responsibility and nature, since God and Satan are evenly matched—but God ultimately must prevail.

4. Harry Wells, *The Failure of Psychoanalysis*, pp. 70, 210.

5. "The Revolutionary Character," in *The Dogma of Christ*, p. 163.

6. Review of C. G. Jung, *Memories, Dreams, Reflections, Scientific American*, CCIX, 33 (September, 1963), 286.

7. *The Revolution of Hope: Toward a Humanized Technology*, p. 13.

8. Cited by Lewis Chester, *Sunday Times* (London); reprinted in *Lansing State Journal*, August 4, 1968, B-4. For a critical account of Maccoby's study see Daryl J. Bem, *Beliefs, Attitudes, and Human Affairs* (Belmont, Calif., 1970), pp. 19-21. Bem's principal criticism is that the biophile-necrophile description is self-evidently biased, predetermining "good guys and bad guys." This criticism could also be applied to many of the categories in Fromm and Maccoby's *Social Character in a Mexican Village*, discussed elsewhere.

9. Robert S. Lynd and Helen Merrell Lynd, *Middletown in Transition: A Study in Cultural Conflicts* (New York, 1937), pp. 490-91. Similar conclusions, based on the assumptions underlying popular humor, were reached by Don Hausdorff in "Topical Satire and the Temper of the Early 1930's," *The South Atlantic Quarterly*, LXV (Winter, 1966), 21-33.

10. The literature on the role of the media is, of course, immense. A good range of attitudes can be found in Floyd W. Matson and Ashley Montagu, eds., *The Human Dialogue: Perspectives on Communication* (New York, 1967).

11. "Mother," 76-77.

12. "Psychoanalysis," in James R. Newman, ed., *What is Science?* (New York, 1955), p. 363. On this basis, Fromm argues for example that love, or respect, is not just a "religious and philosophical idea. The study of neurosis proves empirically that they are the necessary condition of sanity."

13. Ernest Nagel, "Methodological Issues in Psychoanalytic Theory," in Sidney Hook, ed., *Psychoanalysis: Scientific Method and Philosophy* (New York, 1960), pp. 39-40.

14. S. Stansfeld Sargent and Marian W. Smith, "A Brief Epilogue," *Culture and Personality*, pp. 213-15.

15. J. A. C. Brown, *Freud and the Post-Freudians*, p. 5.

16. Carl Rogers, "The Loneliness of Contemporary Man," in Ruitenbeek, p. 33; Rollo May, "The Context of Psychotherapy," in Ruitenbeek, pp. 72-73, 81, 90.

17. Abraham Maslow, *Toward a Psychology of Being*, p. vi.

18. See in particular *The Crisis of Psychoanalysis*, pp. 15-20.

19. Quoted in Richard Heffner, "An Interview with Erich Fromm," 132-33, 213-18.

20. "Epilogue," *The Crisis of Psychoanalysis*, p. 159.

Selected Bibliography

PRIMARY SOURCES

1. Books.

The Art of Loving. New York: Harper, 1956.

Beyond the Chains of Illusion: My Encounter with Marx and Freud. New York: Trident, 1962.

The Crisis of Psychoanalysis: Essays on Freud, Marx, and Social Psychology. New York: Holt, Rinehart & Winston, 1970.

The Development of the Dogma of Christ (1931). Translated in *The Dogma of Christ and Other Essays on Religion, Psychology, and Culture.* New York: Holt, Rinehart & Winston, 1963.

Escape from Freedom. New York: Holt, Rinehart & Winston, 1941.

The Forgotten Language: An Introduction to the Understanding of Dreams, Fairy Tales and Myths. New York: Rinehart, 1951.

The Heart of Man: Its Genius for Good and Evil. New York: Harper & Row, 1964.

Man for Himself: An Inquiry into the Psychology of Ethics. New York: Holt, Rinehart & Winston, 1947.

May Man Prevail? An Inquiry into the Facts and Fictions of Foreign Policy. Garden City, N. Y.: Doubleday, 1961.

Marx's Concept of Man (With a Translation from Marx's Economic and Philosophical Manuscripts by T. B. Bottomore). New York: Frederick Ungar, 1961.

The Nature of Man (ed., with Ramón Xirau). New York: Macmillan, 1968.

Psychoanalysis and Religion. New Haven, Conn.: Yale University Press, 1950.

The Revolution of Hope: Toward a Humanized Technology. New York: Harper & Row, 1968.

The Sane Society. New York: Holt, Rinehart & Winston, 1955.

Sigmund Freud's Mission: An Analysis of His Personality and Influence. New York: Harper, 1959.

Social Character in a Mexican Village: A Sociopsychoanalytic Study (with Michael Maccoby). Englewood Cliffs, N. J.: Prentice-Hall, 1970.

Socialist Humanism: An International Symposium (ed.). New York: Doubleday, 1965.

War Within Man. New York: American Friends Service Committee, 1963.

170 ERICH FROMM

You Shall Be as Gods: A Radical Interpretation of the Old Testament and its Traditions. New York: Holt, Rinehart & Winston, 1966.
Zen Buddhism & Psychoanalysis (with D. T. Suzuki and Richard De Martino). New York: Harper, 1960.

2. Articles and Other Short Writings.

Omitted are some brief items which essentially recapitulate what Fromm has written elsewhere. Publications in German are listed under their English titles.

"Afterword," to George Orwell, *1984.* New York: New American Library, 1961, pp. 265-75.
"The Application of Humanist Psychoanalysis to Marx's Theory," in Fromm, ed., *Socialist Humanism.* New York: Doubleday, 1965, pp. 207-24.
"Are We Sane?" in Walter D. Nunokawa, ed., *Human Values and Abnormal Behavior.* Chicago: Scott, Foresman, 1965, pp. 64-70.
"Authority and the Family," in Max Horkheimer, ed., *Sozialpsychologischer Teil.* Paris: Felix Alcan, 1936, pp. 77-135, 230-38.
"The Case for Unilateral Disarmament," *Daedalus,* LXXXIX (1960), 1015-28.
"The Contribution of the Social Sciences to Mental Hygiene," in Alfonso Millan, ed., *Proceedings of the Fourth International Congress on Mental Health.* Mexico City: La Prensa Médica Mexicana, 1952, pp. 38-42.
"A Counter-Rebuttal [to Herbert Marcuse]," *Dissent,* III (Winter, 1956), 81-83.
"The Crisis of Psychoanalysis," in *The Crisis of Psychoanalysis: Essays on Freud, Marx, and Social Psychology.* New York: Holt, Rinehart & Winston, 1970, pp. 1-29.
"Do We Still Love Life?," *McCall's,* XCIV (August, 1967), 57, 108-10.
"Faith as a Character Trait," *Psychiatry,* V (1942), 307-19.
"The Feeling of Powerlessness," *Zeitschrift für Sozialforschung,* VIII (1937), 95-119.
"Foreword," to A. S. Neill, *Summerhill: A Radical Approach to Child Rearing.* New York: Hart Publishing Co., 1964, pp. ix-xvi.
"Freud's Model of Man and Its Social Determinants," in *The Crisis of Psychoanalysis: Essays on Freud, Marx, and Social Psychology.* New York: Holt, Rinehart & Winston, 1970, pp. 30-45.
"A Global Philosophy of Man," *The Humanist,* XXVI (July/August, 1966), pp. 121-22.
"The Human Implications of Instinctivistic Radicalism," *Dissent,* II (Autumn, 1955), pp. 342-49.

"Humanistic Planning," in *The Crisis of Psychoanalysis: Essays on Freud, Marx, and Social Psychology.* New York: Holt, Rinehart & Winston, 1970, pp. 59-68.

"Individual and Social Origins of Neurosis," *American Sociological Review*, IX (1944), pp. 380-84.

"Introduction," to Patrick Mullahy, *Oedipus: Myth and Complex— A Review of Psychoanalytic Theory.* New York: Hermitage, 1948, pp. i-vi.

Let Man Prevail: A Socialist Manifesto and Program. New York: McCall Associates [1960].

"Man is Not a Thing," *Saturday Review*, XL (March 16, 1957), 9-11.

"Man-Woman," in Margaret M. Hughes, ed., *The People in Your Life: Psychiatry and Personal Relations.* New York: Knopf, 1951, pp. 3-27.

"Marx's Contribution to the Knowledge of Man," in *The Crisis of Psychoanalysis: Essays on Freud, Marx, and Social Psychology.* New York: Holt, Rinehart & Winston, 1970, pp. 46-58.

"Medicine and the Ethical Problem of Modern Man," in *The Dogma of Christ and Other Essays on Religion, Psychology, and Culture.* New York: Holt, Rinehart & Winston, 1963, pp. 175-94.

"The Method and Function of an Analytic Social Psychology" (1932), in *The Crisis of Psychoanalysis: Essays on Freud, Marx, and Social Psychology.* New York: Holt, Rinehart & Winston, 1970, pp. 110-34.

"Mother," *Psychology Today*, IV (March, 1971), 74-77.

"The Oedipus Complex: Comments on the Case of Little Hans," in *The Crisis of Psychoanalysis: Essays on Freud, Marx, and Social Psychology.* New York: Holt, Rinehart & Winston, 1970, pp. 69-78.

"The Oedipus Myth," *Scientific American*, CLXXX (1949), 22-27.

"On the Problems of German Characterology," *Transactions of the New York Academy of Science*, V (1942-43), 79-83.

"The Prophetic Concept of Peace" (1960), in *The Dogma of Christ and Other Essays on Religion, Psychology, and Culture.* New York: Holt, Rinehart & Winston, 1963, pp. 209-18.

"Psychoanalysis," in James R. Newman, ed., *What is Science?* New York: Simon & Schuster, 1955, pp. 362-80.

"Psychoanalysis—Science or Party Line?" in *The Dogma of Christ and Other Essays on Religion, Psychology, and Culture.* New York: Holt, Rinehart & Winston, 1963, pp. 135-48.

"Psychoanalysis and Zen Buddhism," in Erich Fromm, D. T. Suzuki, and Richard De Martino, eds., *Zen Buddhism & Psychoanalysis.* New York: Harper, 1960, pp. 77-141.

"Psychoanalytic Characterology and its Application to the Understanding of Culture," in S. Stansfeld Sargent and Marian W.

Smith, eds., *Culture and Personality.* New York: Viking, 1949, pp. 1-12.

"Psychoanalytic Characterology and its Relevance for Social Psychology" (1932), in *The Crisis of Psychoanalysis: Essays on Freud, Marx, and Social Psychology.* New York: Holt, Rinehart & Winston, 1970, pp. 135-58.

"The Psychology of the Criminal and of Punishing Society," *Imago,* XVII (1931), 226-51.

"The Real Menace of Fascism," *Science Digest,* XII (August, 1942), 34-38.

"Remarks on the Problem of Free Association," *Psychiatric Research Reports, 2.* Washington, D. C.: n.p., 1956, pp. 1-6.

Review of C. G. Jung, *Memories, Dreams, Reflections, Scientific American,* CCIX (September, 1963), 283-88.

Review of Richard M. Brickner, *Is Germany Incurable? Saturday Review of Literature,* XXVI (May 29, 1943), 10.

"The Revolutionary Character," in *The Dogma of Christ and Other Essays on Religion, Psychology, and Culture.* New York: Holt, Rinehart & Winston, 1963, pp. 151-71.

"Robert Briffault's 'Mothers,'" *Zeitschrift für Sozialforschung,* II (1933), 382-87.

"The Sabbath," *Imago,* XIII (1927), 223-34.

"Selfishness and Self-Love," *Psychiatry,* II (1939), 507-23.

"Sex and Character," *Psychiatry,* VI (1943), 21-31.

"Should We Hate Hitler?," *Journal of Home Economics,* XXXIV (1942), 220-23.

"The Significance of the Theory of Mother Right for Today," in *The Crisis of Psychoanalysis: Essays on Freud, Marx, and Social Psychology.* New York: Holt, Rinehart & Winston, 1970, pp. 79-83.

"The Social Background of Psychoanalytic Therapy," *Zeitschrift für Sozialforschung,* IV (1935), 365-97.

"The Social Philosophy of 'Will Therapy,'" *Psychiatry,* II (1939), 229-37.

"The State as Educator," *Zeitschrift für pa. Paedagogik,* III (1930), 110-30.

"The Theory of Mother Right and Its Relevance for Social Psychology" (1934), in *The Crisis of Psychoanalysis: Essays on Freud, Marx, and Social Psychology.* New York: Holt, Rinehart & Winston, 1970, 84-109.

SECONDARY SOURCES

So much has been written about the many ideas discussed by Fromm that any bibliography has to be highly selective. This list includes only those items about Fromm which make substantial or provocative comment. Allusions and references in the text itself should provide useful clues for continued and deeper investigation.

BIRNBACH, MARTIN. *Neo-Freudian Social Philosophy.* Stanford, Calif.: Stanford University Press, 1961. Balanced, sensible study; examines social and political ideas in Fromm, Sullivan, Horney, Kardiner, Alexander and Lasswell; Fromm receives the most attention.

BRAMS, JEROME. "From Freud to Fromm," *Readings in Psychology Today.* Del Mar, Calif.: Communications/Research/Machines, Inc., 1967. Comparison of basic approaches to theory and therapy of Freud ("primarily the psychologist") and Fromm ("more the social philosopher"); sympathetic to Fromm's "humanism."

BRIGGS, ASA. "From Slaves to Robots," *New Statesman and Nation,* LI (June 23, 1956), 739. Thoughtful review of *The Sane Society.*

BROWN, J. A. C. *Freud and the Post-Freudians.* Baltimore: Penguin, 1961. Informed, no-nonsense overview by astute British psychiatrist.

CHASE, RICHARD. "Psychoanalysis at Dead Center," *Partisan Review,* XVIII (1951), 119-24. Well-known literary critic's review of *Psychoanalysis and Religion* surrounded by fervent assault on "Neo-Freudianism."

"*Escape from Freedom*—A Synoptic Series of Reviews," *Psychiatry,* V (1942), 109-34. Positive and negative comments by many scholars: Thomas Harvey Gill, Ruth Benedict, Anton T. Boisen, Lewis B. Hill, Patrick Mullahy, M. F. Ashley Montagu, Lewis Wirth, Ernest E. Hadley.

EVANS, RICHARD. *Dialogue with Erich Fromm.* New York: Harper, 1966. Not really a "Socratic dialogue," as the author suggests, but an exposition and summation of Fromm's positions in response to the interviewer's questions. Some good clarification and occasional modification of ideas expressed through the years.

FRIEDENBERG, EDGAR. "Neo-Freudianism and Erich Fromm," in Hendrik M. Ruitenbeek, ed., *Psychoanalysis and Contemporary Culture.* New York: Delta, 1964, pp. 376-90. Lucid critique which neither damns nor exalts revisionists but attempts to extract that which is most valid and significant.

GREEN, ARNOLD W. "Sociological Analysis of Horney and Fromm," *American Journal of Sociology,* LI (1946), 533-40. Sociologist Green is unhappy with Horney's and Fromm's sociology; advises them to stay inside boundaries of psychoanalysis and concentrate on helping individual patients.

GREGOR, A. JAMES. "Erich Fromm and the Young Karl Marx," *Studies on the Left,* III (1962), 85-92. Review of *Marx's Concept of*

Man; argues that Fromm overemphasizes earlier "idealistic" writings.

H. P., "The Insane Society," *Dissent*, III (Winter, 1956), 84-89. Review of *The Sane Society*.

HEFFNER, RICHARD. "An Interview with Erich Fromm," *McCall's*, XCIII (October, 1965), 132-33, 213-19. Fromm's views about current questions of marriage, rearing children, sex, and war.

HERBERG, WILL. "Freud, the Revisionists, and Social Reality," in Benjamin Nelson, ed., *Freud and the 20th Century*. New York: Meridian, 1957, pp. 143-63. A religious scholar prefers Freud to Fromm, but finds some of Fromm's ideas are useful correctives.

HERTZ, RICHARD C. "The Spiritual Odyssey of a Man of Science," *Detroit News*, November 20, 1966, 3C. Review of *You Shall Be as Gods*.

HYMAN, STANLEY EDGAR. "Psychoanalysis and the Climate of Tragedy," in Nelson, cited, pp. 167-85. On basic rightness (and literary utility) of Freud's picture of man and basic failure (and literary inadequacies) of revisionists.

JAMES, WALTER T. "Karen Horney and Erich Fromm in Relation to Alfred Adler," *Individual Psychology Bulletin*, VI (1947), 105-16. An Adlerian finds Adler seminal to much of Horney's and Fromm's thought.

JOSEPHSON, ERIC AND MARY. Introduction to *Man Alone: Alienation in Modern Society*. New York: Dell, 1962, pp. 9-53. Psychological, philosophical, and literary overview in which Fromm is seen as important theorist.

KARIEL, HENRY. "The Normative Pattern of Erich Fromm's *Escape from Freedom*," *Journal of Politics*, XIX (1957), 640-54. Fromm's conception of politics seen as resting on postulated, but unproven, norms of human needs and drives.

KECSKEMETI, PAUL. "The All-Powerful 'I,'" *Commentary*, XXI (February, 1956), 176-78. Ways in which Fromm does or does not connect with religious concepts.

MARCUSE, HERBERT. "A Reply to Erich Fromm," *Dissent*, III (Winter, 1956), 79-81. Third item in exchange with Fromm about meaning and nature of Freud's (and Fromm's) radicalism.

————. "The Social Implications of Freudian 'Revisionism,'" *Dissent*, II (Summer, 1955), 221-40. Portion of Marcuse's *Eros and Civilization* charging that Fromm and other "Neo-Freudians" "mutilated" trenchancy and radicalism of Freudian theory.

MASLOW, ABRAHAM H. *Toward a Psychology of Being*. Princeton, N. J.: Van Nostrand, 1962. Paralleling recent books by Rollo May, Gordon Allport, and others, presents theory resembling Fromm's in some significant aspects.

MATSON, FLOYD. *The Broken Image: Man, Science and Society*.

Garden City, N. Y.: Doubleday, 1966. Unorthodox intellectual history of recent times, with Freudian revisionism one of many topics placed in context.

MENNINGER, KARL. "Loneliness in the Modern World," *Nation*, CLIV (March 14, 1942), 317. Review of *Escape from Freedom*, sharply critical of Fromm's revisions of Freud.

MENNINGER, ROY W. "Comments," in Fromm, *War Within Man*. New York: American Friends Service Committee, 1963, pp. 36-37. Bound together with text, together with criticisms by Paul Tillich, Hans Morgenthau, and others. One of the famed psychiatric family believes that Fromm equates "death" itself with "badness."

MULLAHY, PATRICK. *Oedipus: Myth and Complex—A Review of Psychoanalytic Theory*. New York: Hermitage, 1948. Clear, readable survey of the theories of Freud and his successors. At this time, Sullivanite Mullahy was much impressed by Fromm.

—————. "Philosophical Anthropology vs. Empirical Science," *Psychiatry*, XVIII (1955), 399-409. After *The Sane Society* with its attacks on Sullivan's conception of "self" and love, Mullahy felt Fromm had deviated too far from scientific method.

PERCY, WALKER. "The Coming Crisis in Psychiatry," *America*, XCVI. Part I: January 5, 1957, 391-93; Part II: January 12, 1957, 415-18. Among other things, Percy is troubled by absence of any religious dimension in Fromm's concept of "transcendence."

PETUCHOWSKI, JAKOB J. "Erich Fromm's Midrash on Love," *Commentary* (December, 1956), 543-49. Examination of Hebraic roots of *The Art of Loving*.

PFEUTZE, PAUL E. *Self, Society, Existence: Continuity in the Thought of Martin Buber and George Herbert Mead*. New York: Harper, 1961. Little on Fromm per se, but pertinent for numerous parallels about ideas of human and "spiritual" feeling and communication.

RIEFF, PHILIP. *Freud: The Mind of the Moralist*. New York: Doubleday, 1961. Excellent study of Freud, published at about same time as Fromm's *Sigmund Freud's Mission*; noteworthy here because of similarities and differences in treating some of same topics.

RIESMAN, DAVID. *Individualism Reconsidered and Other Essays*. New York: Free Press, 1964. Along with considerable analysis of *The Dogma of Christ*, essays contain numerous indications of approaches closely allied to Fromm's.

SARRO, RAMÓN. "The Interpretation of the Oedipus Myth According to Freud and Heidigger," *Journal of Existential Psychiatry*, I (1961), 478-500. Fromm's Oedipal theory noted, in context with more famous ones.

SCHAAR, JOHN H. *Escape from Authority: The Perspectives of Erich Fromm.* New York: Harper, 1961. First full-length study of Fromm's work. Schaar, a political philosopher, finds Fromm unscientific, self-contradictory, and overly ambitious in his aspirations.

SEELEY, JOHN R. "The Americanization of the Unconscious," in Charles Rolo, ed., *Psychiatry in American Life.* New York: Delta, 1966, pp. 142-55. Consideration of the "socializing" of Freud's instinct theory by "Neo-Freudians."

SYKES, GERALD. *The Hidden Remnant.* New York: Harper, 1962. Good, dispassionate discussion of Fromm, as well as chapters on Horney, Sullivan, and others.

THOMPSON, CLARA. *Psychoanalysis: Evolution and Development.* New York: Thomas Nelson & Sons, 1950. Associate of Harry Stack Sullivan offers "inside" view of "Neo-Freudian" theories and methods of therapy; finds Fromm's role significant.

TILLICH, PAUL. "Erich Fromm's 'The Sane Society,'" *Pastoral Psychology* (September, 1955), 13-16. Admiring many of Fromm's methods and conclusions, eminent theologian feels absence of guiding spiritual sense.

WELLS, HARRY K. *The Failure of Psychoanalysis—From Freud to Fromm.* New York: International Publishers, 1963. Systematic critique of major principles of psychoanalytic theory by Pavlovian psychologist. Title indicates author's conclusion.

Index

DATE DUE

MAY 1 '80	MAY 5 '80		
MAY 5 '80	MAY 15 '80		
GAYLORD			PRINTED IN U.S.A.